In trouble and in joy

Other titles by Sharon James

My heart in his hands
*Ann Judson of Burma: a life with selections
from her Memoir and letters*

God's design for women
*Biblical womanhood
for today*

IN TROUBLE AND IN JOY

Four women who lived for God

— With selections from their writings —

SHARON JAMES

EVANGELICAL PRESS

EP BOOKS
Faverdale North, Darlington, DL3 0PH, England

web: http://www.epbooks.org
e-mail: sales@epbooks.org

133 North Hanover Street
Carlisle, PA 17013, USA

www.epbooks.us
e-mail: usasales@epbooks.org

First published 2003
Second printing 2004
Third printing 2011

British Library Cataloguing in Publication Data available

ISBN-13: 978-0-85234-546-7   ISBN-10: 0-85234-546-1

Printed and bound in Great Britain by the MPG Books Group

To Lydia

Contents

Acknowledgements

I am very grateful to those friends and relatives who have read, corrected and commented on all or parts of this book. My father suggested that I work on Margaret Baxter; Dr Michael Haykin suggested that I work on Anne Steele; Mr David Chalkey encouraged me to work on Frances Ridley Havergal. My thanks to each, as well as to those who have given or lent me books related to this project.

I am thankful to Mr Taylor and the staff at the Evangelical Library, London, and to Mrs Susan Mills of the Angus Library, Regents College, Oxford for help in locating sources.

Thanks are due to the Principal of Regents College, Oxford, the Rev. Dr Paul Fiddes for permission to quote from the Steele Collection, and to Dr Karen Smith for allowing me to use her unpublished MPhil thesis on the Calvinistic Baptists of Hampshire and Wiltshire. Alan and Joan Fielden of Pastelwood Studio, Wellington, kindly provided the painting from which the illustration of Apley Castle is taken.

I am indebted to Janice Van Eck for her editorial work, her work on the layout and illustrations, and for her ongoing encouragement.

As always, my husband Bill provided both spiritual inspiration and technical help; our children Peter and Lydia ensured that the days of writing were injected with humour and humanity; and it is a privilege to be part of the church family at Emmanuel. My thanks to you all.

Sharon James
Leamington Spa, August 2003

Introduction

This book looks at the lives and writings of four women who lived between the seventeenth and the nineteenth centuries in England and America. At first sight it would seem that they had little in common.

Their family situations were very different. Margaret Charlton was the fashionable, wealthy, beautiful teenager who married the much older Puritan preacher Richard Baxter. They never had children, and Margaret used her considerable talents and energy working alongside her husband. Sarah Edwards was a devoted wife and mother of eleven children. Anne Steele and Frances Ridley Havergal both refused offers of marriage and remained with their respective fathers and stepmothers: family life being a positive experience for Anne Steele, but in later years a most trying experience for Frances Havergal.

They lived in totally different contexts. Margaret Baxter lived through the English Civil War. Her childhood experience of being attacked by Parliamentarian soldiers traumatized her for life. She suffered (albeit brief) imprisonment with her husband. She saw gross poverty and squalor in London and ministered in situations of appalling need. Sarah Edwards lived in a quiet New England town for much of her life, but when war broke out some of her near neighbours were scalped by native Americans and she had soldiers billeted in her back garden. By contrast, Anne Steele remained in the same peaceful English village, and Frances Ridley Havergal was always based in pleasant and genteel English towns.

They would have been used to quite different styles of worship. Margaret Baxter organized clandestine preaching meetings and knew firsthand what persecution was like. Sarah Edwards experienced revival in the packed-out Congregational church in Northampton, but later worshipped alongside native Americans in a primitive meetinghouse on the frontier. Anne Steele composed her hymns for the simple services of a quiet village Baptist chapel in Wiltshire. Frances Ridley Havergal, a staunch Anglican, loved choral cathedral services.

Something they did have in common was that each was (relatively) privileged; each belonged to the class that used the labour of the poorer classes in domestic service. Not that this made life easy for any of them. It would be inconsistent to criticize them for acquiescing in the economic and social divides of their time when our own standard of living depends on the grossly underpaid labour of those in the developing world. In two hundred years' time our own blind spots may amaze our descendants.

Of course, if they had in common a relatively privileged social situation, they shared the restrictions imposed on women. Each was intellectually gifted. But further education or a profession was barred to them: women were expected to marry and have children. Until Margaret Charlton married, she suffered intense depression. No careers were open to her, and she lacked direction. Once she married, her depression lifted: her calling would now be to support her husband's ministry. Sarah Edwards fulfilled the Puritan ideal in marrying and having a large family. She seems, however, to have found the continual physical demands intensely challenging. Sarah was intellectually gifted and of a mystical temperament. Her unremitting domestic responsibilities left little space for solitude and reflection. This seems to have caused tension, expressed in physical illness and emotional depression, which was only resolved by an intense spiritual experience at the time of the revival in Northampton. Anne Steele managed to stay single, despite proposals of marriage and the urging of her family, and carved out something of a writing career for herself. Frances Ridley Havergal also found her niche in writing, although she had to work with constant interruptions, and never had the opportunity of a place she could call her own in which to work. An increasing number of women in the eighteenth and nineteenth centuries were finding that writing was something that was acceptable for women. It could be done in the privacy of home and thus achieved without women leaving their 'proper' sphere.

Most notably, throughout the wide range of situations these four women experienced (war, insecurity, persecution, loss of health and bereavement), they shared a common perspective. Their contentment and happiness did not depend on good health, a fulfilling job, or a happy family life. It came from living for God. We shall see that each one was genuinely able to praise God through the bad times as well as the good.

In each case, I have given something of the historical setting, then outlined the story of the woman's life, and then assessed her character and significance. At the end of each section is a selection of extracts from that woman's writings, to allow her to speak in her own words. The style and content vary greatly: there are journal entries, resolutions, letters and poems. Some of the selections are deeply religious; others are just fun. The extracts range from the dense seventeenth-century prose of Margaret Baxter's resolutions, which give an authentic taste of Puritan devotion, to the chatty friendliness of Frances Havergal's letters. This book therefore provides a selective anthology of female writing from the seventeenth to the nineteenth century.

As with any anthology, readers can pick and choose. Some may want to read the biographies and leave the original writings. Others may want to read the stories followed by the relevant selections. Or you can work through the biographies and turn to the numbered extracts to illustrate the story at the appropriate point (references to the relevant extracts are given throughout the biographical sections).

Biography is always provisional — dependent on the available sources. These women have given me some surprises. I never imagined that the wife of the great Puritan Richard Baxter was a rebellious (and glamorous) teenager who was converted under his ministry when he was in his forties, and who ended up proposing to him. She seemed to suffer from an eating disorder — something many assume was unique to a later age. It was reassuring to find that Sarah Edwards, wife of the great revival preacher, was human enough to struggle with issues of thinking too much about what others thought of her husband's ministry. I was astonished to discover letters and poems by Anne Steele that showed her to have a sparkling sense of humour, and which belied the solemn impression I had of her from her hymns. Frances Havergal was disarmingly frank about her enjoyment of life, as well as extraordinarily resigned to intense suffering. And as more sources come to light, there may be more surprises. Each was a real human being, not a figure in a stained-glass window, but each one of them was totally consecrated to God.

I have enjoyed getting to know them. I hope you do too.

Through all the changing scenes of life,
  in trouble and in joy,
  the praises of my God shall still
  my heart and tongue employ.

O magnify the Lord with me,
  with me exalt his name;
  when in distress to him I called,
  he to my rescue came.

Of his deliverance I will boast
  till all that are distressed
  take comfort from God's help to me
  and find in him their rest.

The hosts of God encamp around
  the dwellings of the just;
  deliverance he provides for all
  who in his mercy trust.

O taste his goodness, prove his love!
  Experience will decide
  how blessed are they, and only they,
  who in his truth confide.

Fear him, you saints, and you will then
  have nothing else to fear;
  his service shall be your delight,
  your needs shall be his care.

Nahum Tate (1652–1715) & Nicholas Brady (1659–1726)
© In this version, Praise Trust

Timeline

1600

1620   Pilgrim Fathers land in New England

1625

1639

1642–1649   English Civil War

1650

Margaret Baxter

1660   Charles II crowned

1675

1681

1688   'Glorious Revolution' – some freedom for Nonconformists to worship in England

1700

1710

1717

Sarah Edwards

1725

1744   War between France and England – hostilities in North America

1758

Anne Steele

1750

1775

1776   Declaration of Independence (USA)

1788

1789   French Revolution

1800

1825

1836

1837   Queen Victoria crowned

Frances Ridley Havergal

1850

1861–1865   American Civil War

1875

1879

1900

MARGARET
BAXTER

1639–1681

Margaret's birthplace, Apley Castle, near Wellington
(from a painting by Joan Fielden)

Key dates & places

1615 Birth of Richard Baxter

1639 Birth of Margaret Charlton

1644 Apley Castle sacked during the Civil War

1655 Move to Kidderminster

1659 Conversion

1662 Marriage to Richard Baxter

1681 Death of Margaret

1691 Death of Richard

Shrewsbury

Birmingham

Kidderminster

London

England

*M*argaret Baxter's life was one of fascinating contrasts: strong courage in the face of persecution; fearful anxiety when confronting illness. The intense love between her and Richard Baxter is one of the great love stories of church history, and her admirable initiative runs counter to the lingering stereotype of Puritan female passivity. She was born in 1639[1] into a wealthy and respected English family. In 1662, aged twenty-three, she married Richard Baxter — a nationally known Puritan minister then aged forty-seven. Their nineteen years of marriage coincided with the period of vicious persecution for those, such as Baxter, who could not, or would not, conform to the newly established state church. Despite harassment and even a brief imprisonment, they enjoyed a wonderfully happy marriage. When Margaret died at the premature age of forty-two, Richard was broken-hearted, but immediately wrote an account of her life as a catharsis for his grief: an astonishingly frank account of a companionate marriage.

The setting

The mid-seventeenth century saw England torn by civil war. Family members were divided; as were close friends. Those of piety and integrity were found on both sides. Many had their lives turned upside down. Charles I was executed in 1649. Oliver Cromwell ruled as 'Lord Protector' from 1653 until his death in 1658. During this brief period there was freedom for Puritans, such as Richard Baxter, to minister. When Cromwell died, there was general unease at the succession of his embarrassingly incompetent son Richard.

Charles II returned to rule England in 1660. Although he had promised that the convictions of Puritan clergy would be respected, about two thousand ministers were ejected from their parishes in 1662. The ensuing years saw cruel persecution of those whose consciences would not allow them to conform to the state church. John Bunyan was the most famous of those who were imprisoned for preaching without an official licence. He survived imprisonment. Others did not. The 'Glorious Revolution' of 1688 ended this terrible time — Catholic James II fled the country, to be succeeded by William III and Mary his wife. Shortly afterwards, in 1689, to the great joy of Nonconformists, the Act of Toleration granted them freedom of worship.

The period of Richard and Margaret Baxter's married life (1662 to 1681) almost exactly coincided with the years of persecution: they suffered imprisonment on one occasion, and were in constant fear of arrest.

Their married life began and ended in the capital. By 1700 one in nine of the population lived in London (about 400,000); many parts were overcrowded, filthy and dangerous. A fifth of Londoners suffered an agonizing death in the 'Great Plague' of 1665. The next year (four years after the Baxters' marriage) saw the destruction of the central city by the 'Great Fire'. But the very poorest slums, outside the city limits, were not burned, and thus not rebuilt. Conditions in these were wretched: the smell overpowering, disease rife and infant mortality high. It is likely that only one child in four born in London during this time survived.

As if plague, fire and gross poverty were not enough, Londoners faced the constant threat of invasion. The English were intermittently at war with the Dutch (1652–1654; 1665–1667; 1672–1674). There were fierce naval battles off Lowestoft (1665), and Dover (1666). In 1667 the Dutch sailed up the Thames and Medway and bombarded Chatham. Rumours of invasion abounded. It is not surprising that Richard commented that Margaret was often tormented by fear because of the talk of massacres.

Richard Baxter

Before turning to the life of Margaret, we will give a brief overview of the life of her husband, Richard Baxter (1615–1691). He has been described as 'the most truly eminent English churchman of his century.'[2] This is the more astonishing, as he was mainly self-taught. He was born in Rowton, Shropshire, in 1615 into a respectable yeoman family (neither genteel nor poor). His father could not afford to send him to university; he received some education from tutors, and then was sent to court at the age of eighteen. He had already experienced something of a religious awakening, and the frivolity of court life sickened him. He returned home and set himself to study theology. At the age of twenty-four, he was ordained by the Bishop of Worcester, and became an assistant minister at Bridgnorth. In 1641, aged twenty-six, he took up a curacy in Kidderminster. He ministered there among humble handloom weavers until 1660, except for an interlude during the Civil War when he ministered to the Parliamentary army.

Baxter played a leading role in the recall of Charles II, but he had fundamental doubts about episcopacy, and when he was offered the bishopric of Hereford, he declined. When the Act of Uniformity was passed on St Bartholomew's Day, 24 August 1662, any minister who could not accept every part of a revised Prayer Book had to leave the Established Church. This was a terrible defeat for those, such as Baxter, who had urged a flexible policy of comprehension. He had hoped, for example, that those who had scruples about such things as making the sign of the cross in the baptism service could still be accommodated in the church. About 2,000 ministers were ejected from their parishes, and by default became Nonconformists.

For the next thirty years, Baxter's ministry was mainly one of writing, though he became an unofficial leader among the Nonconformists, respected both because of his massive intellect and his transparent godliness. Whilst ministering at Kidderminster he had worked for as much unity as possible between Episcopalians, Presbyterians and Independents, and demonstrated the same irenic spirit after 1662. He declared himself to be a 'mere Nonconformist': in other words he was reluctant to be labelled as a Presbyterian or a Baptist or a Congregationalist. He would have preferred to be back in the Church of England, but only if parish clergy were allowed freedom in their own parishes to order their own services.

Baxter's greatest contribution to the English church was his nearly two hundred written works. Some have become enduring classics, such as the *The Saints' Everlasting Rest*, and *The Reformed Pastor*. His *Christian Directory* contained over a million words, and addressed every area of practical Christian living.

Baxter was not content to limit his ministry to writing. He wanted to preach, and risked persecution and imprisonment by doing so. He was appallingly treated by the authorities, imprisoned, fined, had two valuable libraries confiscated and was viciously insulted by the notorious Judge Jeffreys because of 'sedition' contained in one of his books published in 1685.

Baxter applauded the overthrow of the Catholic James II and the succession of William and Mary in 1688, but he died in 1691, aged seventy-six, only two years after the Act of Toleration.

The story

Eventful childhood, rebellious youth
(1639–1656)

In 1644 Margaret Charlton, aged just five years old, cowered with fear as Parliamentarian troops sacked her home. The Charltons had lived at Apley Castle, near Wellington, in Shropshire for three centuries. Margaret's father, Francis Charlton, had died in 1642, and her mother, Mary, had remarried the following year. Margaret's stepfather was a Royalist named Hanmer. In 1644 the Parliamentarians sacked the castle, imprisoned Hanmer, and seized over £3,000 of property. Little Margaret witnessed part of the castle burned to the ground, men killed, and all of the inhabitants, including herself and her family, terrorized and stripped of their clothing. Memories of this terrible incident haunted her for the rest of her life. To make matters even more traumatic, it seems that family rivalry lay behind the attack. Margaret's mother was determined to protect the interests of her young son, Francis, and would not let his uncle (Robert Charlton, the next male in the line of inheritance) have custody. It seems that this uncle engineered the siege of Apley Castle by the Parliamentarians. Following the siege, Robert Charlton took custody of the children. Mrs Hanmer managed to get them back again, and keep them, although Robert did not give up his efforts to gain custody. Margaret and her siblings must have found the emotional insecurity of this tussle between their mother and uncle extremely traumatic.

Meanwhile, Margaret's future husband, Richard Baxter, had been curate of the quiet parish of Kidderminster for just a few months when he found himself accused of 'treachery' by Royalist sympathizers in the town. The 'fury of the rabble' forced him to leave.[3] He witnessed the carnage of Edgehill, then took refuge in the Parliamentary garrison at Coventry for some time. He was deeply disturbed at the extremism of many on the Parliamentary side. In 1645 he resolved to exert what moderating influence he could, and became an itinerant minister with the Parliamentary army. His horror at the bloody scenes of war, his disillusionment with the side he supported, his empathy with the national angst, all inspired what may be his greatest work: *The Saints' Everlasting Rest*.

After the war, Baxter's ministry back in Kidderminster (1653–1660) was astonishingly fruitful — even by Puritan standards. Kidderminster was a market town, serving about twenty villages in the surrounding countryside. The parish was made up of about eight hundred families: between three and four thousand people, many of them were involved in the weaving industry. When Richard first arrived, there was hardly one family on each street who were 'godly'. The combination of Baxter's powerful preaching ministry and intensive pastoral visiting transformed the situation. By the time he left, there were some streets where there were fervent Christians in virtually every home. Baxter was often offered more prestigious positions, but he was determined to serve the humble weavers of that small parish for the rest of his life.

In 1655, Margaret's mother moved to Kidderminster in order to sit under the ministry of this gifted preacher. Her second husband had died, and she had looked after Apley Castle on behalf of her son Francis until his own marriage in 1655. It seems that there were disputes between Francis and herself. Her older daughter had married and moved to Oxford; Margaret, the younger daughter, stayed with her mother. Mary Hanmer was a pious woman, and disturbed by the frivolity and worldliness of her younger daughter. Like many teenagers, Margaret was chiefly concerned with socializing, romance and fashionable clothes. Her mother appointed a religious governess, but this was counterproductive, as the strictness of this woman only served to alienate Margaret still further from religion. When Mary decided to move to Kidderminster she had no idea that her daughter would not only be converted under Baxter's ministry, but would also become his wife.

The very notion of this happening would have seemed wildly improbable to the forty-year-old Richard Baxter when sixteen-year-old Margaret and her mother moved to Kidderminster. Baxter believed that if a pastor was serving as assiduously as he ought to, there would be no time for the responsibilities of married life. He waxed eloquent on the subject, and his views were well known.

If Richard was a sworn bachelor, then Margaret was a confirmed flirt, and vain with it. She was disgusted at the poverty and dreariness of the humble inhabitants of Kidderminster. In rebellion against the move she reacted by dressing as splendidly and ostentatiously as possible.[4]

A change of heart (1656–1662)

Outward rebellion concealed an inner turmoil. The prayers of Margaret's mother were answered. Despite herself, Margaret found that under Richard's ministry she was forced to face up to her own selfishness and pride. She became convinced that she was guilty before God of terrible sin. Her analysis of her sins became almost an obsession. After her death Richard discovered the 'self-judging' papers she wrote at this time (*extract 1*). She admitted to her diary that she questioned the truth of the Bible, that she was selfish and proud and that she could not bear people who had different views from her own.

Looking back, one can see that alongside the process of accepting the Christian message, Margaret was definitely falling for the messenger. Indeed, there seems to have been a certain inevitability about her feelings for him, given that it was from Richard that Margaret sought spiritual counsel. In modern terms she was receiving highly intense one-to-one counselling from him — albeit normally in the form of letters. One of the sins for which she reproached herself was an over-attachment to 'the means of grace', a thinly disguised reference to her pastor.

When Margaret was twenty, in 1659, she finally professed conversion. Before that time there had been clear evidence of a changed life. Shortly after this she became critically ill. The inner stress of her conversion, plus the turmoil of her growing attachment to the avowedly celibate pastor may have had something to do with her vulnerability to infection. Richard and some of the other parishioners decided to set aside time to fast and pray for her recovery. They experienced great fervency in their prayers — she was wonderfully healed.[5]

When she had recovered, her mother invited those who had prayed for her to keep a day of thanksgiving. Richard asked Margaret what they should especially give thanks for. In true Puritan fashion she gave him seven points of thanksgiving, and five requests (*extract 2*). Later her husband found a secret covenant, written at the same time (*extract 3*).

Her private journal reveals her deep sense of unworthiness. She made many strict resolutions. She determined to avoid rich foods and parties, and luxuries of any kind (*extract 4*). After recovering from her critical illness she was left with a legacy of regular severe headaches (possibly migraines) and severe respiratory problems (possibly asthma). It is not altogether surprising that Margaret was often depressed, tense and fearful. It is impossible to say how much of this was due to physical and genetic factors, how much was due to intense anxiety about her sins, and how much was due to her growing affection for the unavailable pastor. Obsessive worry was exacerbated by her inability to communicate her feelings to others: she would bottle her fears up rather than discussing them and getting them back in perspective.[6] Her natural reserve meant that she was often misunderstood.[7]

Following her illness and recovery, Margaret developed a great fear of losing her reason. An aunt of hers had suffered mental illness, and her parents had tended towards instability. Margaret was naturally excitable, and her very fear of insanity tended to push her closer to the edge. Richard commented:

Her understanding was so far from failing, that it was higher and clearer than other people's; but, like the treble strings of a lute, strained up to the highest, sweet, but in continual danger...[8]

Margaret Baxter

Richard Baxter's pastoral care for all within his parish was superlative. His book *The Reformed Pastor* (based very much on his own practice) is the classic on the subject. He demonstrated the pastoral care to Margaret that he showed to all his parishioners; but evidently there was an increasing affection between them.

In 1660 Charles II was restored to the throne. Baxter left for London in April to play his part in the establishment of a restored Church of England. He lodged for the next couple of years with an old friend. Margaret was desolate after Richard left for London (*extract 5*). She and her mother followed him, taking lodgings near to where he was staying — despite his efforts to dissuade them. The next January, Margaret's mother died. Margaret had been totally devoted to her, but now she really was alone in the world. Richard preached the funeral sermon on 30 January 1661. We can speculate that Richard would have drawn alongside Margaret as he attempted to comfort her in her loss. There is no firm evidence of when he began to feel deeply for her, but it could have been during this difficult time.

One source indicates that Margaret took the initiative and proposed to him, and that a secret and lengthy engagement ensued. James Anderson quotes this story in his 1862 work *Memorable Women of the Puritan Times*, but does not give a source. It is tempting to dismiss this extraordinary scene as apocryphal, but who knows? Anderson writes:

> *The spark of love to his person was kindled in*
> *her heart. The attachment was ultimately recip-*
> *rocal, but as may be inferred from allusions in*
> *several passages of his Breviate of her life, it*
> *began on her part. At first she closely concealed*

it from others... But the passion caused her an aching languishing of heart, and this acted so injuriously upon her feeble frame as even to endanger her life. At last she made it known to Baxter that while he was ministering to her soul, there had sprung up in her bosom, and mingled with her religious concern and devotional feelings, an affection for his person, which she could not repress. 'She being a pious and devout young lady' says a nearly contemporary writer, 'fell in love with him upon account of his holy life and fervency of preaching, and therefore sent a friend to acquaint him with her respects in his chamber. His answer was, That since he had passed his youth in celibacy, it would be reputed madness in him to marry a young woman, whilst he could not discharge the duties of a husband in all respects. She at the door, over-hearing, entered the chamber and told him, "Dear Mr Baxter, I protest with a sincere and real heart, I do not make a tender of myself to you upon any worldly or carnal account, but to have more frequent converse with so holy and prudent a yoke-fellow, to assist me in my way to heaven, and to keep me steadfast in my perseverance, which I design for God's glory and my own soul's good." Mr Baxter was at a stand, and convinced that with a good conscience he could not despise so zealous a proffer, springing from so pure a fountain of love.' Yet after they had agreed upon marriage, their union was delayed for a considerable period, from causes which Baxter does not particularly specify.[9]

It is unclear what Margaret did during the next eighteen months. Baxter was fully occupied in negotiations regarding the future of the Church of England. In June he became one of Charles II's chaplains, and in July he preached before the king. In the autumn he was offered a bishopric, but declined it. He still hoped against hope that the national church would be inclusive of those with Puritan convictions. To his dismay, a Bill for Uniformity in the church became more and more rigid as it progressed through Parliament. It became law in May 1662. Conscientious objection meant that nearly two thousand clergy had to leave their parishes (and their means of financial support). Baxter preached his farewell sermon in London shortly after the act received royal assent. This was a heartbreaking time — it signalled the end of the ministry he loved. He was silenced, but he was free of bitterness. From then on, every Sunday, he invariably attended the service at a parish church (and tried to look for something good in the sermon).

An unlikely marriage (1662)

Baxter's removal from ministry brought with it one great blessing. No longer in pastoral ministry, his justification for celibacy was removed. He married Margaret on 10 September 1662.

The marriage took place after what had been, for Margaret at least, years of suspense. Clearly she had become devoted to him, and longed to marry him. Baxter's biography of Margaret originally included a full account of their courtship — sadly for us, friends persuaded him to omit this.[10] We can only guess that the delays caused Margaret enormous tension — a situation hinted at in her journal (*extract 6*).

Gossips had a wonderful time when the news broke. The marriage caused a stir: partly because of the age gap (Richard was then forty-seven and Margaret was twenty-three); partly because he had been so outspoken in his former determination to remain unmarried; and also because of his poverty. Baxter asked Margaret to agree to three conditions before they married. Firstly, he would not have any claim on any of her property, so that he would not be criticized for marrying her for her money. Secondly, he would not become involved in any lawsuits resulting from her inheritance. Finally, she was not to be demanding of his time. If he wanted to devote himself to preaching or writing, she was not to complain about it.[11]

Living with Margaret was the chief consolation enjoyed by Baxter during the following grim years. His whole life had been focused on parish ministry. Now his *raison d'être* was cruelly stripped away. He was a natural pastor — without a parish; a born preacher — without a pulpit. He grieved intensely. But Margaret was always there for him: comforting him, caring for him in his frequent illnesses, shouldering all of the practical concerns of life. He poured his huge desire to minister and his immense energy into writing. His productivity was proverbial even in his own day: a total of 128 books in addition to countless letters, articles, and prefaces to the books of other writers. This was made possible, in part at least, by Margaret's loyal and loving care.

Marriage to Richard transformed Margaret's social and economic status — for the worse. Instead of wealth she faced persecution and insecurity. But she was overwhelmingly happy. She was now married to the one she loved and admired more than anyone she had ever met. Her depression lifted. Her emotional insecurity vanished. She was content.[12] If Richard seemed to have lost his *raison d'être*, she had found hers. She now had a purpose in life. Her parents were dead and, as a single woman, there was no career open to her. But she believed in Richard's calling and was overjoyed at the prospect of supporting him in it. She never put pressure on him to conform to the state church, even though this would have spared both of them much suffering.

Richard silenced (1662–1672)

The first year of marriage was spent in Moorfields, a pleasant wooded country area to the north of London. Baxter was unable to preach at all, even in private meetings. He devoted himself to writing, but was continually interrupted by a stream of visitors. He decided to move further out into the country, where he could write without distraction. For six years he and Margaret lived at Acton (in Middlesex), six miles outside London. During this time they moved at least once, maybe twice. Wherever they lived, Margaret made a great impression through her thoughtfulness and kindness. Always popular with her neighbours because of her generosity, she also showed concern for their spiritual well-being, and gave away literally hundreds of books to any who would read them.[13]

Both Margaret and Richard must have found these first years of marriage to be a challenge. Richard gives a glimpse of the adjustment called for when he commented that he had always considered it a sinful waste of time to keep stairs and rooms as clean as dishes and could not understand Margaret's obsession with neatness and cleanliness. But he realized that her careful ordering of the household was actually widely praised, and a product of her background.

Moreover, his comments on marriage in *A Christian Directory* (comments written just a couple of years after his own marriage), suggest that he may have been taken by surprise at how much time was needed to calm her anxieties and reassure her fears. Richard here sounds positively chauvinistic, but we must bear in mind that by the end of his nineteen years of marriage with Margaret he was more than ready to confess her quite his equal:

> *And it is no small patience which the natural imbecility [weakness] of the female sex requireth you to prepare... Women are commonly of potent fantasies, and tender, passionate, impatient spirits, easily cast into anger, or jealousy, or discontent... And the more you love them, the more grievous it will be, to see them still in discontents...*[14]

For her part, Margaret had fallen in love with her pastor, and now she had to adjust to living with the real man: usually ill, sometimes bad-tempered, and sometimes offhand with her. Both needed great reserves of patience. Richard wrote in the *Directory* that husband and wife needed to avoid everything that tends to quench love in the other. It seems that despite the differences in age, background and temperament, they each managed to put the interests of the other first, and build a truly happy partnership.

Many of the inhabitants of Acton died during the 'Great Plague' of 1665. Richard was staying with a friend (Richard Hampden) in Buckinghamshire when it broke out. It seems likely that Margaret urged him to stay there until the danger was over: he was away from late summer 1665 until the following March. When he returned home, so many fresh graves had been dug that the churchyard looked like a ploughed field. Large numbers of his neighbours had died, but all his family had survived. It seems that Margaret remained at Acton during this time, and if so would certainly have ministered to her sick and grieving neighbours. When the 'Great Fire' ravaged London in 1666, the Baxters witnessed the flames from where they lived. Richard the writer was particularly struck by seeing the charred pages of burnt books, which blew as far as Acton.

Regular family devotions were a feature of these years, and the Baxters opened their home to neighbours. This was risky. In 1664 the Conventicle Act banned all religious meetings that did not use the Prayer Book where there were five people in addition to a single family. During one private 'service' a bullet was fired though a window, narrowly missing one woman's head. Despite this, numbers grew, and the Baxters moved to a larger house.

Throughout these years, the Baxters loyally attended the parish church. But Richard's ministry in his own home compared rather too favourably with the local curate's — a weedy youngster who spent most of his time in the ale-house. In June 1669, six years after Richard and Margaret had moved to Acton, Baxter was arrested. When he refused to take the non-resistance oath (promising not to attempt any alteration of government in either church or state), he was sentenced to six months' imprisonment in the New Prison, Clerkenwell. When he sued for *habeas corpus* (the right not to be imprisoned without a fair trial) it was discovered that there was a technical fault in the warrant for his imprisonment. He was thus released after a brief imprisonment of between one and three weeks.

Ever the loyal and loving wife, Margaret insisted on joining him in prison. A kind jailor allowed them a large room, access to a garden, and even allowed Margaret to bring in an assortment of their possessions including their best bed. She did her best to make prison accommodation more pleasant and 'homelike'. Richard later commented: 'I think she had scarce ever a pleasanter time in her life than while she was with me there.'[15]

On release, they could not risk returning to Acton. Richard would have been arrested again, and there was talk of imprisoning him in the common jail at Newgate: a vile place with a high death rate. It seems that a friend gave them temporary refuge, while they searched for a place to live at least five miles from Acton or London. (The so-called 'Five Mile' Act prohibited Nonconforming preachers from preaching, or even coming within five miles of a place where they had previously ministered unless they could swear the non-resistance oath). Eventually, some months later, they found lodgings in Totteridge, near Barnet, in Hertfordshire (today, this is in the Greater London area). Here they remained for about three years.

At first they rented a section of a poor farmer's house. It was miserably smoky, and Margaret's breathing problems were exacerbated. 'We were even suffocated in the stink',[16] commented her husband. Even here, Margaret's characteristic generosity surfaced, and she managed to give the poor landlady money for an apprenticeship for her son. Despite her many moves, Margaret managed to take a personal interest in those around her wherever they lived. Moreover, her happiness in being married to Richard meant that the inconvenience of constant moves seemed secondary.[17] She simply got on with organizing the practicalities, for Richard was a typical academic, and hopeless on the everyday realities of life.

In the summer of 1670, the Baxters moved into a large

house of their own. Richard's eighty-year-old stepmother came to share their home. Then Margaret invited two close friends, Mr and Mrs Corbet, to come and live with them as well. She and Frances got on immensely well, and after Mr Corbet died, Frances stayed with the Baxters until Margaret's death. The Corbets, like the Baxters, had been driven from London by the Five Mile Act, and like them had taken refuge in Totteridge.

The new home, though large, was in need of a great deal of renovating. Margaret had her hands full organizing alterations and improvements. As ever, Richard devoted himself to his writing: he was at his most productive in Acton and Totteridge. But Margaret did not allow him to isolate himself in his study. She reminded him of his duties to catechize the servants regularly, and of the need to be gracious and patient with visitors.

We should not think that these were peaceful years. Richard was the object of constant slander. When anyone wanted to write against the Nonconformists, it seemed they used his name as the object of their scorn, knowing that he did not have the freedom to reply for himself. Moreover he was deprived of freedom of movement: if he went anywhere near London, or Acton, he risked arrest under the Five Mile Act. If he were arrested again, it was likely that he would be imprisoned in Newgate. With his precarious health, he almost certainly would not survive.

Promoting Richard's preaching ministry — the hardships of Nonconformity (1672–1681)

King Charles II had given assurances before his restoration to the throne that religious persecution would not take place. In flat contradiction to this, Parliament had pushed ahead with strict enforcement of the Act of Uniformity. The king was never happy about this. He disliked religious persecution, and on 15 March 1672, he issued a Declaration of Indulgence. This suspended the penal laws in force against both Protestant Nonconformists and Catholics. Baxter and many others reacted with mixed feelings. Now they could preach without fear of imprisonment. But they did not welcome being treated on equal terms with Catholics. In addition, Baxter was not really interested in 'toleration'. He wanted *comprehension* — to be accommodated *within* the established church. Baxter also disapproved of the king's acting unilaterally without Parliament. He was realistic enough to know that Parliament would soon find a way of thwarting this new toleration. He was right. From March 1672 licences were granted to Nonconformist ministers and meeting places, only to be recalled by Parliament in the following year.

By then, however, the Baxters had moved back into London. They did not move back as soon as indulgence was declared. They wanted those ministers who had stuck it out in the capital during the grim years of fire and plague to establish themselves and gain congregations first. Moreover, on principle, Baxter did not want to apply for a licence to preach if this meant he had to declare himself to be an Independent, Presbyterian or Anabaptist. Eventually he wrote applying for a licence as a 'mere Nonconformist'.[18] The licence was granted. In November 1672 Baxter preached openly for the first time in ten years. This took place in his own home rather than in a church, much to his sorrow. He still longed to be accommodated in the Established Church, but would not compromise his principles. Soon he was invited to London to give four lectures at Pinner's Hall. In January 1673 he began preaching on Fridays at a meeting place in Fetter Lane.

At this point Margaret seems to have put pressure on Richard to move to London to preach to a wider audience. She found a large and pleasant house in Southampton Square, and they moved in after Easter 1673. For the remaining eight years of her life, she saw it as her ministry to support, encourage and sometimes badger him to continue in the precarious occupation of being a Nonconformist preacher.

In 1673 the Declaration of Indulgence was rescinded. But what happened to the licences that had been granted to individual preachers? There was confusion as to whether these were still valid. In practice many Nonconformists went on preaching. Margaret was certainly determined that Richard should continue to preach. When they arrived in London she felt that he was not moving fast enough to minister. First, he wrote, she 'fished out of me' which place he really wanted to preach in. He told her that St Martin's was a parish with 40,000 more than could fit in the available churches, and multitudes who lived like savages.[19] The most needy area within St Martin's was called St James'. On her own initiative Margaret went out and hired a room over St James' marketplace, persuaded Richard to preach there every morning, secured an assistant minister, employed a clerk and a female caretaker, and covered many of these expenses herself. It was in this meeting place that tragedy nearly occurred, and it was Margaret's presence of mind that averted it.

On 5 July 1674, while 800 people were listening to her husband in the upper room, the main supporting joist began to crack. Panic broke out. Richard urged everyone to stay calm and remain where they were. Margaret rushed downstairs, summoned the first man she met, found that he was a carpenter, and begged him to put a temporary support in place. The man lived close by, had a handy prop, and came and saved the meeting. Later investigation showed that a real tragedy had been averted. Gratitude and relief prompted Margaret to make two vows to God: a vow to give public thanks, and a vow to build a safer meeting place. She was, however, shaken by the whole incident: indeed her husband believed that she never recovered her emotional equilibrium.

Richard continued to preach at St James' until the lease expired a few months later. After that, he would have been content with occasional preaching opportunities, especially as his health was failing. But Margaret had made a promise to God. She could not break it. Shortly after this she rented a site nearby in Oxendon Street, and raised money to build a meeting place.

It was while she was organizing this, in June 1675, that a warrant was granted to confiscate £50 of Baxter's goods. Margaret ensured that Richard's books were safely disposed of: sold, given away or loaned. It is one of the heartbreaking aspects of persecution that an inveterate reader such as Baxter was separated from his books for such lengths of time. When he left Kidderminster in 1660, he had to leave his extensive library behind. For thirteen years it suffered the ravages of rats and bookworms. He only recovered it when he resumed ministry in 1673, and then had to disperse it through fear of confiscation two years later. Despite all this, over 1,400 volumes were left in his library on his death.[20]

Harassment continued. In August 1675, Richard was due to stay with a friend in Hertfordshire for a few weeks, to escape the worst of the summer heat. When word came through that his arrest was imminent, his friends forced him to leave immediately for the comparative safety of Hertfordshire. The next Sunday — only the second time the new Oxendon Street meeting place was used — a visiting speaker took his place. This man had been warned of the risks, and sure enough, three Justices of the Peace arrived with a warrant for Richard's arrest. In his absence, they imprisoned the visiting speaker instead. Margaret provided for the unfortunate man while he was in prison and paid his legal fees. Meantime Richard was vilified as if he had deliberately allowed someone to be arrested in his place.[21] He refrained from preaching for six months, but Margaret was not put off ministering in the area. She began a school for poor children; no fees were charged, and she begged money off her friends to keep it going.

Nor was she deterred in her efforts to ensure Richard's continuing preaching ministry. She rented out the Oxendon Street meeting place to the parish church, and hired another room on Swallow Street — another poor area. Here Baxter preached for about six months, from April to November 1676. Then, once again, officers were sent to prevent him from preaching. It was Baxter personally whom they objected to: Margaret arranged for other preachers to come to Swallow Street for some years afterwards. When he was finally driven from that area, he wrote, 'It was her choice that I should go to Southwark, each Lord's day to preach to a congregation of poor people there.'[22]

Altogether Margaret raised money to build several chapels. This was done through private approaches to Christian friends: she abhorred public collections in case the poor were embarrassed. Margaret was open-handed, and expected others to be the same. She was most displeased if friends did not give freely when she asked them to. If ever she saw a person in need she could not resist offering to help, and then did the rounds of her friends — who must have come to dread her visits! Richard tried to moderate this tendency. Generosity was all very well, but he firmly believed that a little more prudence and discernment was needed. When he expressed this view, she accused him of being mean.[23] The chief cause of tension between them was that he had persuaded her to give up her claim to so much of her estate, so that she was unable to relieve the poor to the extent she would have liked.

The final illness (1681)

Since her critical illness in her late teens, Margaret had feared losing her reason. There was some family history of mental instability, but there were also the various stresses she endured, which pushed her dangerously close to irrationality.[24] Richard listed these stresses, including the sack of the family home by soldiers during the Civil War, her critical illness, fire next to their house, the near collapse of the church she had rented, the 'Great Plague', the 'Great Fire of London', many other fires nearby and rumours of massacres. Little wonder that her sleep was often disturbed by nightmares. She was easily startled, and often fearful. Richard attributed this more to physical than spiritual factors, and he did not think it involved moral guilt. Rather, he saw it as an evidence of grace that so naturally timid a person enjoyed such a strong assurance of her own faith.

Three years before her death, she lost touch with reality for a few days. Richard reckoned that this was partly due to anxiety, partly due to a friend's persuading her to take powdered ginger every morning![25] From that time on,

Margaret suffered intense pain in one of her breasts. Several of her friends and relations had died of cancer. She became convinced that she was suffering from breast cancer, and that she would soon die. Richard could not believe that this was the case. He was in a miserable situation. Margaret became upset if he told her she would be fine — she became equally distressed if he played along with her and agreed that she was probably going to die. At any rate, she prepared herself for death.[26] It was fear of cancer that led her to starve herself. For many years she would only allow herself a little milk or water with some chocolate in it morning and night, with a few pieces of meat at dinner time.[27]

About ten weeks before her final sickness the pain moved to her right kidney, and Margaret tried drinking 'Barnet waters' and taking 'tincture of amber'. Far from being helped, she got worse, and eventually lapsed into delirium. When the doctors followed the common practice of bleeding her, this probably destroyed what little strength she still had.[28] After twelve days of intense illness, she died on 14 June 1681 aged forty-two. Three days later, on the 17th of June, she was buried in the grave she had built for her beloved mother.

Her character and significance

The Puritan movement of the seventeenth century laid the doctrinal foundation for the Protestant church in the English-speaking world. Whereas the medieval Catholic Church taught that salvation depended on taking the sacraments and being part of the institutional church, the Puritans emphasized individual conversion and relationship with God. Each Christian needed to possess assurance of salvation: hence the importance of personal Bible reading and prayer, listening to good preaching, journal keeping and examination of one's spiritual state. Margaret Baxter epitomized all of this — as is seen in her covenant, resolutions and notes of personal examination. Her determination to promote Richard's preaching ministry illustrated the Puritan confidence in preaching. The medieval Catholic Church had exalted celibacy, but the Puritans exalted marriage and family life, regarding the Christian home as a little church. Richard Baxter had regarded celibacy as ideal for a minister, but his own marriage changed his mind. Margaret worked right alongside him as 'a partner in the gospel'. After she died, his written testimony of his love for his wife was so powerful that the Baxter marriage was often lifted up as 'the ideal' for others to admire and follow (*extracts 7 & 8*).

Richard and Margaret never had children. This enabled Margaret to devote her time and energy to gospel work. She was an inveterate evangelist. She always encouraged her husband and other preachers they knew, and she willingly opened her home to any who would come in to listen to preaching. Such courage was remarkable. The risk of imprisonment was real. Several Nonconformists died in prison during this period, for conditions were atrocious. Shortly after her death Richard was arrested and treated with shameful cruelty and contempt.

Margaret was competent and capable, and took the burden of everyday life off her husband. He freely admitted that in many matters (especially practical) he deferred to her better judgement. He confessed that he was not able to cope with household matters. It had not mattered so much when he was single. After he married, she took the burden of domestic affairs, and he was glad to leave it like that.[29] Even in pastoral matters, unless there was a really complex theological issue involved that demanded a high degree of learning, he deferred to her judgement. Unless they were strictly confidential, he ended up sharing all pastoral problems with her:

> She was better at resolving a case of conscience than most divines that ever I knew in all my life. I often put cases to her, which she so sud-denly resolved, as to convince me of some degree of oversight in my own resolution... Abundance of difficulties were brought to me, some about references, some about vows, some

about marriage promises, and many such like;
and she would lay all the circumstances
presently together, compare them, and give me
a more exact resolution than I could do.[30]

Margaret was determined to support Richard's preaching ministry; she was devoted to evangelism; she had a deep compassion for the poor. She was willing to spend all they had (and more) to relieve the deep needs around them.

Her popularity with her neighbours was due to her cheerful and pleasant demeanour, which she managed to keep up even when consumed with anxiety. This is a remarkable testimony to her unselfishness. It is simply not true that the Puritans went around looking miserable. Indeed, Richard Baxter wrote, 'Keep company with the more cheerful sort of the godly; there is no mirth like the mirth of believers.'

Margaret was endlessly patient in her dealings with others. This could be a cause of tension between them when Margaret would bear with hopeless cases for years and Richard would advocate a sterner attitude.[31] She was much more patient and generous with numbers of Richard's poor and demanding relatives than he was. She was not tempted to anger, and always spoke calmly and gently — he was notoriously quick-tempered (and she reproved him for it!). She was not aggrieved by their sufferings, and reproved Richard for speaking openly of them.[32] She refused to hear negative talk of the conformists.

But she could not hide the other side of her character from Richard. Margaret was an idealist and a perfectionist. Her expectations were unrealistic. She wanted to experience a constant state of spiritual fervour. She not only made unreasonable demands upon herself, she demanded too much of her husband and others. Richard was positive about her quest for holiness, but we can guess that it could be hard to live with:

> *She was very desirous that we should all have lived in a constancy of devotion, and a blameless innocency. And, in this respect, she was the meetest helper that I could have had in the world ... for I was apt to be over careless in my speech, and too backward to my duty; and she was still endeavouring to bring me to a greater wariness and strictness in both. If I spoke rashly or sharply it offended her.*[33]

If her husband neglected his manners, she told him. If his very expression was unpleasant (for example when he was very ill) she would tell him too! She reminded him if he failed to catechize the servants. When in later years he suffered from a whole catalogue of illnesses, and was understandably less communicative, she berated him.[34] If constant weakness and pain meant that he prayed less regularly with her, she was not happy about that.

Richard admitted that his wife was over-zealous about the spiritual well-being of others. She could not bear it if they did not match up to her very high standards.[35] She was offended when Richard seemed uncommunicative, hasty or impatient.[36]

Richard confessed that Margaret's scrupulous fear of hypocrisy meant that she probably spoke far less of spiritual things than she should have done. She would not even lead family prayers when he was away as other wives would have done.

He also conceded that some were critical of his wife. She should — they said — have stayed meekly at home instead of being so busy with the church and good works.[37] In answer, he pointed out that Paul named women as his helpers in the gospel. Others complained that she was so open-handed with her money that when she died she left her husband in poverty. In answer, Richard pointed out that none of her spending was for her own comfort; indeed she maintained an austere lifestyle.

But he confessed that they did differ over this. He did not think it right to borrow in order to relieve the needs of others. She regularly went into debt in order to relieve need. In admitting that she got her way with regard to philanthropy, was not Richard implicitly saying that she was boss?[38] Some gossips whispered that Richard had abdicated his leadership role. He argued that her benevolence was entirely from her own estate. He compared her generosity to that of Mary who broke the ointment over Christ's feet, and her critics to Judas. He pointed out that Dorcas was commended for open-handed liberality to the poor.

While Richard dismissed the criticisms of others, he was willing to concede that there had been occasional tensions between them. There was some disagreement as to how he should most profitably use his limited strength and resources. She thought he should spend more time in prayers with the household and herself; he should write fewer books, and write those few better. He saw writing as his priority, arguing that there were very few who could do what he was gifted to do. He believed that it was better to write the books imperfectly than not to write them at all.

Margaret tended to take on too much: she was not always wise in realizing her limitations, and this could lead to anxiety and exhaustion. Richard wrote that she spent all she had for God — her material estate, but also her health. Her desire for usefulness overtook her strength.[39] In the end, both mind and body gave way under the strain of her enthusiasm to serve God beyond the energy she had been given. Her premature death, though tragic, was unsurprising.

We see Margaret Baxter as a woman who was prone to anxiety and fear, a woman who suffered nightmares, who had what we would term an eating disorder, who eventually succumbed to the mental illness that she had feared all her life. Moreover we see a woman who was a perfectionist, obsessive, and who drove herself to the limit. But we see also a woman who made a conscious decision to turn away from living for herself, who decided to follow Christ, and who then spent all her energy and her considerable wealth in the service of others.

It is easy to criticize Margaret for her perfectionism, zeal, seriousness and over-sensitive conscience. But if she was hard in her judgements on others, she was harder on herself, and in her dealings with others she was tender and kind. Her compassion for the poor and needy is a shining example, and her almost profligate giving mirrors the very radical teaching of her Saviour.

Margaret lived in cruel times. She loved her husband dearly, and she urged him on in his ministry whatever the cost. She admired him greatly, but was ready to risk telling him his faults if she thought it was for his good. She was fiercely loyal to Richard, but always her highest loyalty was to God. She did not complain at the hardships of being the wife of a Nonconformist minister: insecurity, frequent moves, uncomfortable accommodation, the lack of privacy and the loss of status. Rather, she revelled in the opportunity her marriage gave her to minister: organizing and supporting Richard's preaching, and engaging in philanthropy and educational work. She is especially an inspiring example to ministers' wives. She is also an example to all Christians. For despite natural fearfulness she put Christ first. It did not come easily, and there was often a high price to pay. Margaret exemplified those words that are so easy to sing, but so difficult to live:

Love, so amazing, so divine,
Demands my soul, my life, my all! [40]

Selections from her writings

Extract 1: Self-judging papers

After Margaret died, Richard discovered her private papers. These included the 'self-judging papers' which she wrote around the time of her conversion in 1659. We see here a very typically Puritan emphasis on thorough self-examination: the agonizing analysis of motivation, and the desire to keep an accurate record of one's spiritual progress. She writes down ten marks of the person who has the Spirit of Christ. She then deduces that she does not yet attain this standard. Therefore she is not yet a real Christian.

> Mark 1 – *The Spirit of Christ is the Author of the scriptures, and therefore suiteth your disposition to it, and guideth you by it. I fear then I have not the Spirit of Christ; for I yet feel no love to God's word, nor closure with it as suitable to me, but I am questioning the truth of it, or, at best, quarrelling with it.*
> Mark 2 – *The Spirit of Christ is from heaven,*

from God our Father, and leadeth us upward unto him. Its work is spiritual, of heavenly tendency, making us cry, Abba, Father, and working the heart by uniting love to God. It is not so with me; for I have a spirit tending only to selfishness and sin.

Mark 3 – *The Spirit of Christ uniteth us to Christ, and one another by love, and is against hatred, division, and abusing others. Mine, then, is the spirit of Cain, for I cannot endure any that are not of my opinion and way, and it inclineth me to malice, and unpeaceableness, and division.*

Mark 4 – *The Spirit of Christ is a spirit of holiness, and doth not favour licentiousness in doctrine, or in life. Though I am for strict principles, I am loose in practice.*

Mark 5 – *Christ's Spirit inclineth to love, humility, and meekness, and makes men stoop to each other for their good. None more uncharitable, proud, and censorious than I.*

Mark 6 – *The Spirit of Christ makes men little, low, and vile in their own eyes: it is pride that puffeth up. My self-conceitedness shows that I am unhumbled.*

Mark 7 – *The Spirit of Christ doth work to the mortifying of the flesh, even all its inordinate desires, and to self-denial. I am a stranger to the work of mortification and self-denial. I can deny myself nothing but the comfort of well-doing. I cannot deny my sloth so far as to go to prayer when I am convinced of my necessity.*

Mark 8 – *The Spirit of Christ is a prevailing Spirit, and doth not only wish and strive, but overcome the flesh, as to its rule. The flesh prevaileth with me against the Spirit.*

Mark 9 – Christ's Spirit is the Author of his worship and ordinances, and suits the souls of believers to them, the word, sacraments, etc. They seem not suitable to my soul; I am against them, and had rather not use them, if I durst.

Mark 10 – Christ's Spirit is in all the saints, and inclineth them to holy communion with each other in love, especially to those in whom this Spirit most eminently worketh. It is not thus with me. I desire not the communion of saints; my affections are most to those who are best to me, whether they have more or less of the Spirit.

To go no further, it is now evident that I am a graceless person.[41]

Extract 2: Prayer requests on recovery from sickness

Around the time of her conversion Margaret was critically ill. Richard and others fasted and prayed, and she was healed. The people who had prayed followed up with a day of thanksgiving. Richard asked Margaret what she wanted them to give thanks for, and she gave him the following written points:

My life hath been a life of very great mercies, and these have aggravated my sin in overlooking them. Some of those which God hath most affected my heart with, I shall here mention; but, alas! with a heart very insensible of the greatness of them.

1. *My mother's restoration I would first thank God for; and next, for many mercies of mine own. Four times before this I have been delivered from great danger of death.*

And now I desire to acknowledge his mercy in delivering me from this death-threatening disease, and that in answer to prayers I am here now in competent health to speak of the goodness of the Lord.

2. *I desire to acknowledge it a mercy that God afflicted me; and though I cannot, with the psalmist, say, 'But now I keep thy statutes;' I can say, 'Before I was afflicted I went astray.'* And how many great sins God hath prevented by this affliction, I cannot tell; but am sure that God hath dealt very graciously with me; and I have had many comforts in my sufferings which God hath not given to many of his beloved ones.

3. *I desire to acknowledge God's great mercy to me in bringing me to this town under such useful means of grace; and that at such a time when I was even ready to engage in a course of sin and vanity, beyond what I had formerly lived in.* This mercy is much greatened by the time; for had the Lord brought me hither in infancy, and removed me at riper years, the mercy would not have been so great. And, if I had gone longer on in a course of hardening sins, it had been less than now it is.

4. *I desire to acknowledge it a great mercy that I want no outward thing, but am enabled to be helpful unto others, and have all the temporal*

mercies that I can well desire, for my encouragement in the ways of God.

5. I desire to acknowledge it a great mercy
that God hath given me an interest in the hearts
and prayers of so many of his faithful servants
in this place.

6. I desire to acknowledge it a great mercy,
that God hath made me the child of godly
parents, and a child of many prayers.

7. I desire to acknowledge it a great mercy,
which I can never be thankful enough for, that
God hath given me a heart in any measure willing to acknowledge his mercies, and be thankful for them; and that, notwithstanding all that
sin and Satan hath done to hinder it, he hath
made me desirous this day to give up myself,
and all that I have, to him; taking him only for
my God and chief felicity.

And now, the requests that I desire you to
make to God, on my behalf, are these:

1. That he will give me a more thankful soul,
that I may praise him all my days.

2. And an humble heart, that I may be taught
of God, who looketh on the proud afar off.

3. And a tender conscience, that I may fear
to offend him, and hate all sin.

4. And strength so to resist temptations, that
I be not led by Satan to dishonour God, or to
provoke him.

5. And a meek and quiet frame of spirit, that
I may be contented to bear the afflictions that
God shall lay me under, without murmuring or
repining.[42]

Extract 3: Secret covenant with God

Many Puritans made a covenant, or commitment, to God at special times. Some would renew this covenant every birthday, or every New Year. When she recovered from sickness Margaret wrote the following, and Richard found it after her death:

This being a day set apart for returning thanks to God, for his mercy in delivering me from the gates of death, these people being they that have earnestly supplicated the throne of grace on my behalf, I here now renew my covenant with Almighty God, and resolve, by his grace, to endeavour to get and keep a fresh sense of his mercy on my soul, and a greater sense yet of my sin. I resolve to set myself against my sin with all my might, and not take its part, or extenuate it, or keep the devil's counsel, as I have done, to the wronging of God, and the wounding of my own soul. I resolve, by God's assistance, to set upon the practice of known duty, and not to study shifts and evasions to put off those which are either troublesome, chargeable, or likely to render me dishonourable and vile in the eyes of the carnal persons of the world. And this I do upon these considerations, and for these reasons:

Yea, God will expect more from me than from many others. Let me, therefore, see that I be in good earnest with God, and think not to put him off with hypocrisy. Let me not deceive myself; for God will not be mocked: what I sow, I shall reap. If I belong to God, though I suffer whilst I am in the body, they will be but light afflictions, and but for a moment; but the ever-lasting kingdom will be mine inheritance; and, when this life is ended, I shall reign with Christ; I shall be freed from sin and suffering, and for ever rejoice with saints and angels. But, should I prove a hypocrite, I lose my labour, I lose my God, and damnation with devils and damned ones will be my reward for ever, and this the greater, as my mercies have been abundant and great.

Therefore, I here desire, this day, to renew my covenant with God, and to beg the prayers of this people, that God will not leave me to myself, but help me, by the sufficient grace of Christ, to keep the covenant which I have made. And I intend to keep this paper by me, to help to remind me, and quicken me to duty, and hinder me from sin, and encourage me to go on cheerfully against temptations, looking still to Christ, who forsaketh not those, that, by faith and repentance, come to him.[43]

Extract 4: Resolutions

It was also common for Puritans to write out resolutions, either on significant dates, such as birthdays, or at times of crisis. Margaret's resolutions made on her recovery included the following:

I resolved to pray and labour for a true sense of the sins of this nation in general and, in particular, of the sins of my relations, and of my own. *And that, till it please God to give me cause of rejoicing on the behalf of my relations, and of my own soul's recovery and spiritual welfare, I will continue with humiliation to supplicate the Lord. And though I would not shut out a greater duty by a lesser, yet I will avoid all manner of feastings as much as I well can, and all noxious sensual delights; and, when I must be present, I will use some mortifying restraint. And this I would do in my habit, and all other things, but that I would lay no snare on myself; by renouncing what occasions may oblige me to; but, by all means, I would strive to keep upon my heart a sense of my friends' danger and my own.*[44]

Extract 5: Richard leaves Kidderminster

Margaret here records her response to Richard's departure to London in 1660. It is an unambiguous indication of the depth of her feelings.

I have now cause of sorrow for parting with my dear friends, my father, my pastor. He is, by Providence, called away, and going a long journey. What the Lord will do with him, I cannot foresee; it may be he is preparing some great mercy for us, and for his praise; I know not but such a day as this may be kept here on his account. The will of the Lord be done, for he is wise and good: we are his own, let him do with us what he pleaseth: all shall be for good to them that love God. I have cause to be humbled that I have been so unprofitable under mercies and

*means, it may grieve me, now he is gone, that
there is so little that came from him left upon my
soul. O let this quicken and stir me up to be more
diligent in the use of all remaining helps and
means. And, if ever I should enjoy this mercy
again, O let me make it appear that this night I
was sensible of my neglect of it... When the Lord
shall take our bodies from the grave, and make us
shine as the sun in glory; then shall friends meet
and never part, and remember their sad and
weary nights and days no more. Then may we
love freely.*[45]

Extract 6: Margaret's love for Richard — and the uncertainty of its outcome

This diary entry hints at the tension suffered by Margaret
in the months, even years, before her marriage. She loved
Richard deeply — but what would be the outcome? And
did her deep love for him threaten to compromise her
love for God?

*I begin already to be sensible of my misusing
the helps which God had given me; I know not
how I should love ordinances and means of
grace, and to what end; not to break my heart
when Providence removeth them from me, or
me from them; but I should love them for God,
and use them for him, and expect my greatest
comfort from him, and not from men and
means themselves. This is no more than what I
thought I had known long ago, but I never knew
it indeed till now. And now I do but begin to*

know it. When I felt my heart ready to sink under a burden of sorrow, God was pleased to ask me what I ailed? Was my condition worse than ever? had I less hopes of his love than heretofore? If not, why do I mourn more than when I lay under that curse? What is it that I have chosen for my hope and happiness? is that lost and gone? Am I left in such a place or case as God cannot be found in if I truly seek him? or that God cannot sweeten with his presence? If not, why do I not contentedly thank God for what I have already had? I cannot say it is better that I had never had it, than now to leave it; no, I must be willing to submit to God, and be humbled in the sense of my abuse of mercy, so far as it may quicken me to diligence for the time to come. And, if ever God more trust me with such treasure as once I had, I will strive to show that I better know the worth of it than I did before.[46]

Extract 7: Richard's love for Margaret — and confidence in the outcome of their love

Richard concluded his memoir of Margaret by quoting from one of his own letters to her. It speaks volumes about the depth and spirituality of their relationship. There is calm certainty that far from compromising their devotion to God, their passionate love for each other is actually a means of grace.

It is our great fault that we are not more skilful and faithful in helping one another, that we might miss each other on better reasons, than

*merely from the inclinations of love. I hope God
will make us better hereafter, that when we are
asunder, each of us may say, I miss the help for
watchfulness and heavenliness, for true love and
thankfulness to God, which I was wont to have.*

*Dear heart, the time of our mutual help is
short, O let us use it accordingly; but the time
of our reaping the fruit of this, and all holy
endeavours, and preparatory mercies, will be
endless. Yet a little while, and we shall be both
with Christ. He is willing respecting us, and I
hope we are willing concerning him, and of his
grace, though the flesh be weak. I am absent,
but God is still with you, your daily Guide and
Keeper; and I hope you will labour to make him
your daily Comfort.*

*And this is the chief comfort which you and
I must have in one another, that is, as helpful
towards God, and as our converse with him will
be durable. The Lord forgive my great unprof-
itableness, and the sin that brought me under
any disabilities to answer your earnest and
honest desires of greater helps than I afford
you, and help me yet to amend it towards you.
But though my soul be faulty and dull, and my
strength of nature fail, be sure that He will be
a thousand-fold better to thee, even here, than
such crooked, feeble, useless things, as is.*

Thy R. B.[47]

Extract 8: 'The Covenant and Confidence of Faith'

In 1681 Richard published *'Poetical Fragments, Written partly for himself, and partly for near Friends in Sickness and other deep affliction'*. He was heart-breakingly honest in the preface. His 'dear companion' having been wrenched away, his 'grief for her removal, and the Revived Sense of former things have prevailed with me to be passionate in the open sight of all'. 'The Covenant and Confidence of Faith' was a poem of eight eight-line verses. Richard had written it on the occasion of Margaret's sickness back in 1659, and Margaret had signed it as the expression of her submission to God's will. Extracts from this poem have been edited into the hymn 'Lord, it belongs not to my care whether I die or live' (*Christian Hymns*, 757). Here are three verses from the original:

My whole, though broken heart, O Lord!
From henceforth shall be thine:
And here I do my Vow record:
This hand these words are mine.
All that I have, without reserve,
I offer here to Thee:
Thy Will and Honour all shall serve,
That Thou bestow'dst on me.

Now it belongs not to my care,
Whether I die or live:
To love and serve Thee is my share:
And this Thy grace must give.
If life be long I will be glad,
That I may long obey:

If short: yet why should I be sad,
That shall have the same pay?

Christ leads me through no darker rooms,
Than He went through before:
He that into God's Kingdom comes,
Must enter by this Door.
Come, Lord, when Grace hath made me meet,
Thy blessed Face to see:
For if Thy work on Earth be sweet,
What will thy Glory be? [48]

SARAH EDWARDS

1710–1758

*Jonathan Edwards' Church, Main Street, Northampton,
by Maitland de Gogorza, Forbes Library, MA.*

Key dates & places

1710   Birth of Sarah Pierrepont

1727   Marriage to Jonathan Edwards

1734–1742   Revival at Northampton — the Great Awakening

1750   Dismissal of Jonathan from the Northampton church

1751   Move to missionary settlement at Stockbridge

1758   Deaths of Jonathan and Sarah

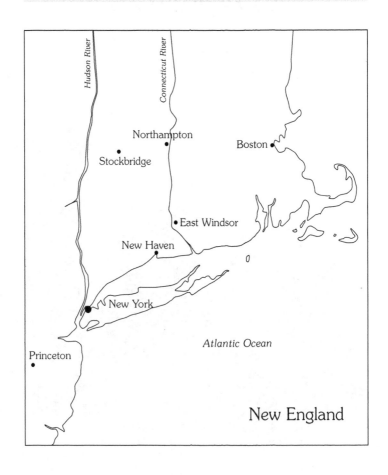

New England

S arah married at seventeen, had her first baby at eighteen, and then had ten more children at more or less two-year intervals until she was forty. She unashamedly devoted herself to her husband, Jonathan Edwards. He was America's foremost revival preacher, and when he set out to describe the religious experience characteristic of a time of revival, he looked to Sarah.

Religious ecstasy is all very well, but it can lead to unpleasant self-righteousness, or practical incompetence in dealing with everyday life.[1] Sarah's experience of God enabled her to face tough times with serenity and contentment. Instead of putting herself above other people, she genuinely put their interests ahead of her own. She was a nicer person to have around as a result of her religious experience. In looking back at what Sarah experienced, we will examine not just what she felt, but how this affected her life in a practical way.

The setting

The Pilgrim Fathers disembarked from *The Mayflower* at
Cape Cod in November 1620. They were the first of
many thousands of English Puritans to settle around
Massachusetts Bay. Fleeing from religious persecution in
the Old World, they hoped to set up a godly nation in the
New. Each town was built around the Congregational
Church, and only church members could hold any civic
position. Living a century after the arrival of these first settlers, Sarah and Jonathan Edwards were to be caught up
in the tension caused as the growing population could not
for ever keep up this ideal of the Christian community.

The greater part of their life was spent in Northampton,
a town of just over 1,000 inhabitants. Its situation was
pleasant: sheltered, with fertile land and beautiful scenery.
Nearly all the families worked the land: men rose at dawn
to work in the fields, or on the constant tasks of felling and
cutting wood (for homes, furniture and fuel). Households
were virtually self-sufficient: many women wove cloth and
made nearly all the goods needed by the family. There was
only one general store. Occasional trips down to Boston

or New York would be necessary for the purchase of luxury goods. There was no mail service and no stagecoach.[2] If you did have to travel, you travelled on horseback along the roughest of roads.

Although life was hard, and restrictive for travel, it was very sociable. Like other New England communities, the settlers chose to live close together, rather than near their own fields. This ensured a close community life, with the church and school as the focal points. Nearly all the settlers would attend church. All men were expected to co-operate if necessary in the defence of the community, all attended military drill and each owned a musket. Each town was self-governing, a little democracy governed by the town hall meeting. The crime rate was virtually zero. It was said that even the plain people of New England were intelligent and refined, in contrast to some oafish settlers of other states whose conversation was restricted to the price of a horse![3]

There was a marked gap between the wealthy and the poor. Church seating was determined by social status. Moreover it was assumed that servants could be bought, sold, and hired out to others. While black slaves faced nothing like the horrors of those labouring in plantations down south, there was still an assumption of their social inferiority. A few (such as the Edwards' close friend Samuel Hopkins) viewed slavery as a horrible evil to be opposed. But the majority, including Jonathan and Sarah, seem to have accepted it as part of the social structure of the day.

The story

Childhood: 'Joy unspeakable'

Sarah Pierrepont was born in 1710 in New Haven. Her father was a well-known minister, James Pierrepont. Her mother Mary (née Hooker) was the daughter and granddaughter of leading ministers. Inhabitants of the New World were just as aware of social status as those in England: Sarah's family was one of the most wealthy and respected in the colony. One of her great-grandfathers was Thomas Hooker, a founder of Connecticut; another great-grandfather was the first mayor of New York.

From a very early age, perhaps even as a toddler, Sarah experienced a sense of God's felt presence.[4] She was only four when her father died, but her mother stayed on in the church where he had ministered for the preceding thirty years. All descriptions of Sarah testify that she was remarkably beautiful, but more remarkable was her deep piety. She was only eight when Jonathan Edwards arrived in New Haven to study at the fledgling Yale College (of which her father had been one of the founders). Sarah's widowed mother had a prominent seat in the church, and it may have been in church that Jonathan was first struck with the piety and beauty of this extraordinary child. Five years later in 1723, when Sarah was thirteen and Jonathan twenty, he penned the description of her that has passed into history (*extract 1*). She loved, he said, to walk alone in the country and think of God. She knew that this Creator God loved her personally and feared more than anything else to offend him. She loved to sing to God, and was always full of joy — sometimes unspeakable joy.

No wonder Jonathan was enthralled, for he had discovered a kindred spirit. From an early age he too had loved to wander alone in the woods and pray; he thought deeply about God, in fact he thought deeply about everything. Tutoring at Yale at the tender age of twenty, he thought and spoke and wrote like a mature professor. No ordinary girl could have suited him. Sarah was extraordinary. She was not disturbed by the profundity of his religious experience, for she shared it. In the absence of any record, we can only wonder what the courtship of two such intense and brilliant youngsters was like.

On 28 July 1727 seventeen-year-old Sarah married twenty-five-year-old Jonathan. In the years to come many people would stay in their home. All spoke with one voice — the deep love and mutual respect of these two individuals was inviolable. They were devoted to each other.

Marriage: 'An uncommon union' (1727)

When Jonathan married Sarah, he had for the preceding five months been co-pastor of the church at Northampton where his grandfather, Solomon Stoddard, had ministered since 1669. At eighty-three, Stoddard was still a forceful preacher, and his church was one of the largest outside Boston. Stoddard's strength of character could lurch into dogmatism — a characteristic that rubbed off on his church members. There was a tendency to party division in Northampton, and arguments in the church had, on one occasion, even ended up with blows. But all seemed reasonably peaceful when the young Jonathan joined his grandfather. He did not appear to have been intimidated by the large number of his own relatives in the congregation, and they in turn seem to have been impressed with their new minister.

Sarah's entry into the church in Northampton in the summer of 1727 was the focus of great excitement. Since the arrival of Jonathan's grandmother in Northampton in 1661, there had not been another minister's wife.[5] Tradition demanded that she wear her wedding dress for her first Sunday service, and turn around slowly so that everyone had a good view. Custom also dictated that she sit every Sunday in a high seat, next to the pulpit, facing the congregation.[6] Total self-control was called for, as any trace of boredom or tiredness would be commented on. Sarah had been used to this intense scrutiny since childhood: her mother had sat in exactly the same honoured and exposed position.

After a few months lodging with Jonathan's grandparents, the young couple moved into their own homestead, a fair-sized house, with ten acres attached and forty acres of farmland further away. Their home became proverbial for hospitality. Most parsonages at that time would have visitors constantly arriving and expecting accommodation, but theirs seems to have been even more welcoming than most. Sarah created a warm, relaxed and happy atmosphere in their home, and stamped her own delightful personality upon it. Her gift was to make every visitor feel special.

From the start of his ministry, Jonathan was unusual. Other ministers were 'people'-orientated — adept at relaxed conversation and seen regularly in the homes of their parishioners. Many ministers worked their own land and engaged in hard physical labour alongside the other townsmen. But Sarah had married no ordinary man. Jonathan Edwards was one of the greatest intellects America has ever known. His whole life revolved around the activities of the mind. Whatever else was going on, even raging on, around him, he was focused on thought, prayer, meditation and writing. He had to have large chunks of time to creatively work through questions of theology, philosophy and what is now called psychology. Although parishioners with problems knew they could call at any time, he generally spent thirteen or fourteen hours each day in his study. There was a sense of destiny about this. God had gifted him with a capacity to push forward the frontiers of thought. He had a solemn obligation to use the talent he had been given. As a young man, Jonathan carefully worked out a regime of diet, exercise and sleep by which he could achieve optimum mental efficiency, and then he stuck to it for the rest of his life. This required iron self-discipline, as he was often ill. Each day Jonathan rose at a punishing hour, usually about 5 a.m., and expected similar hours to be kept by the household.

Instinctively, Sarah understood this. She fitted in with his hours, provided exactly the diet he asked for, nursed him when sick and did not complain when he spent the main part of each mealtime back in the study. She fielded the visitors, the domestic arrangements and the family demands. She did not resent his calling. She supported him unquestioningly because she knew that he loved her unquestioningly. She was absolutely secure. Jonathan spent long hours in the study, but the door was never closed to her. Invariably he would take a break during the afternoon and take her out for a ride in the country; equally invariably he would spend an hour with the family in the evening.

Even more important, Sarah shared her husband's eternal perspective and sense of destiny. Jonathan was not studying for the sake of it. He was convinced that this world is created for a purpose: God's own glory. The establishment of the kingdom of Christ on earth is the means by which this is achieved. His own endeavours in writing and preaching were one little part of the establishment of that kingdom. Sarah believed this implicitly. Her support of his ministry was not only a sign of her love for her husband; she regarded it as service to her God.

But this service had nothing gloomy or threatening about it — the heart of their religion was love. Heaven, wrote Jonathan, is a world of love, and Christians are to begin to live a life of love here too. Christianity is only proved to be real if there is affection, patience, generosity and warmth towards others. Jonathan was a loving husband; Sarah was a loving wife. The great love of God towards them, they believed, demanded no less.

On his deathbed, Jonathan sent word to Sarah that the 'uncommon union' that they had enjoyed for so long could not be broken by death: they would surely love each other through all eternity. Theirs was indeed an 'uncommon union': two extraordinary people, devoted to God and to each other.

Motherhood: A role of eternal significance

The thought of giving birth eleven times without modern pain relief is difficult to contemplate, and despite the enormous reserve with which the subject was treated at the time, Jonathan implied that on at least one of these occasions Sarah's life was in danger. It would be absurd to romanticize the sheer hard work involved in bearing and rearing so many children. We glimpse the pressure in one of the letters written by Sarah's third daughter Esther, when she in her turn was struggling with just two young children [the spelling is her own!]:

> *Now I write with the Son at the Brest — When I had but the one Child my hands were tied, but now I am tied hand and foot. (How I shall get along when I have got 1/2 dzn. or 10 children I cant devize.) I have no help in the House except what is in our Ketchin and you know what that is — our young women are all Ladies and it is beneath them to go out [to domestic service]...*[7]

Sarah's own daughter did not idealize the tedious task of raising a large family, and Sarah's domestic responsibilities would have been unremitting. Certainly she had help in the house, but that was a necessity when everything had to be done at home, even to making up bedsteads each year, taking the frames apart and filling them with fresh straw. Organizing such help was a task in itself. Sarah, like any other woman, found her physical energy depleted with frequent pregnancy and nursing. Sometimes her body gave way. In the winter of 1740 when she was thirty, she and all the children (then aged twelve, ten, eight, six, four, two and six months) had measles. In the traumatic summer of 1750 she succumbed to rheumatic fever.

If the community only saw her bright side — dignity and self-control had been drilled into her since childhood —

Jonathan knew that in the early years of motherhood she was often tense, tired and fearful. Naturally when she was physically weak she was more prone to anxiety. A pernicious result of the equation of church and community was that the minister and his wife were put up on a pedestal. They were accorded a high social status within the town, which meant that they were public property. Sarah was the object of general scrutiny, which must have been difficult when she was suffering from nervous and physical exhaustion. Sunday after Sunday, whatever was going on personally, she had to put on a brave face and take her seat in splendid isolation, a seat which symbolized as effectively as anything else that she was different from the other women in the church. How much more natural (and biblical) if she could have been part of an 'every-member-ministry' type church, with fellow Christians to love and accept her whether she was feeling weak or strong! But we cannot rewrite history. The Edwards were caught up in a social structure that they were powerless to change, even if they had wanted to.

No, Sarah had accepted her situation, and characteristically, she did so by drawing strength from spiritual resources.

She could not change the biological reality that she would bear children for as long as she was fertile. So she deliberately focused on the long term. The short-term perspective involved the pain of childbirth, the reality of sleepless nights, the agony of watching little children suffer from illness, the hard work of discipline. The eternal perspective was that each of her children had an eternal soul. By God's grace, each one would serve him for ever. When her daughter Esther was pregnant with her first child, Sarah took time to write to her of the 'sacred privilege' of motherhood. Even if a child were to die in infancy, it would be worthwhile going through pregnancy and labour. Sarah was sure that the infant would go straight to glory, and have an exalted eternal destiny. Looking back, Esther remembered that her mother had indeed viewed each pregnancy as a gift from God. She prayed for and with each child, and took by far the greatest share of their care.

The other spiritual resource that Sarah drew on to maintain equanimity in the face of the unremitting and unromantic demands of motherhood was an extraordinary sense of the love of God. She came to the point where she handed everything over to God: life or death, health or sickness, wealth or poverty, popularity or rejection. This proved to be totally liberating. When Sarah was thirty-seven her seventeen-year-old daughter Jerusha died. Sarah grieved, but did not despair. She had handed Jerusha over to God: she knew that her daughter was with him.

But, leaving aside eternity, what was Sarah like in the everyday routine of motherhood?

We can catch a glimpse of this from the firsthand accounts written by some of the Edwards' guests. One mid-winter's day in 1741, when Jonathan was away, a complete stranger arrived on the doorstep. Young Samuel Hopkins was going through a spiritual crisis, and believed if anything was going to get him sorted out, then staying with Jonathan Edwards would. Sarah was then thirty-one, and her seven children ranged from thirteen down to eighteen months. She welcomed Samuel in, not just for a week or two but for the whole winter, and from that time on he was a regular visitor and firm family friend. From the first day he was enchanted with Sarah. She was in absolute control of her children (the norm of the time was implicit obedience), but there was also affection and fun.

Day-to-day life was pleasant in their home. Amid all the business of looking after the children, she took time to speak to him about his spiritual anxieties. When Jonathan arrived home, Samuel noted the deep love between husband and wife. The simple and genuine welcome extended to this young student ensured that we have at least a small firsthand glimpse of Sarah as a mother. Other guests supported this testimony. The Edwards' most famous visitor was George Whitefield, who stayed with them in 1740, the year before Samuel Hopkins' arrival. He too was impressed with the harmonious atmosphere in their home. And he too was especially taken with Sarah, and confided to his journal his prayers that God would provide him a partner just like her.

Revival: 'uninterrupted cheerfulness, peace and joy' (1734–1742)

Jonathan Edwards took over as the senior minister at Northampton in 1729, when his grandfather Solomon Stoddard died. The next few years were fairly uneventful. Sarah had given birth to their first child, a daughter called Sarah, in 1728. Three more daughters followed in fairly quick succession: Jerusha, Esther and Mary, who was born in 1734, when her mother was twenty-four.

We have little firm knowledge of Sarah's role in the church. It seems that she was an enthusiastic participant in women's prayer meetings,[8] and we know that she was gifted in drawing people out in spiritual conversation when they visited the parsonage. Sarah never kept a diary, but the diary kept by her third daughter reveals that when Esther married a pastor, Aaron Burr, she immediately began visiting the sick, the poor and the bereaved. This visitation continued even in the busy times after the birth of her children. We may be sure that she was instinctively following the pattern her mother had always set for her. We know that Jonathan Edwards firmly believed in the duty of giving generously to the poor:[9] Sarah was given ample scope to minister to the needy of the parish.

During the first six years in Northampton Sarah settled into the community, and made acquaintance with her husband's numerous relations. Relationships in the large extended family were not always harmonious. In 1734 Jonathan found himself taking the opposite side in a theological conflict from one of his numerous cousins. By itself this should have been totally insignificant. But it wasn't. Israel Williams (aged just twenty-five) never forgave Jonathan, and his hostility was to haunt Jonathan for the rest of his life. It seems likely that Jonathan and Sarah hardly registered the coldness of the Williams, for they were now taken up with a series of dramatic conversions.

By the spring of 1735 Jonathan Edwards reported that he was seeing thirty conversions a week. Three hundred people were converted altogether in a six-month period, in this, the first revival of his ministry. Excitement in the town was intense, and talk was of little else. Jonathan and Sarah found their home crowded with people wanting spiritual advice. Northampton was not the only town affected: similar scenes were taking place in towns throughout Connecticut, and further afield. This widespread religious revival became known as the first 'Great Awakening'. The beginnings of the movement were probably a series of conversions in Dutch Reformed churches in New Jersey in 1726, but then many Presbyterian and Congregationalist churches also saw dramatic increases in membership. Those who had previously been formal or 'nominal' church attenders found themselves gripped by conviction of personal sin, and then wonderfully assured of their personal salvation. A great emphasis was placed on these obvious evidences of an inner work of conversion. But if Jonathan was overjoyed by the three hundred or so conversions, he soon had to cope with the downside of revival.

The mood of Northampton darkened with two appalling suicides. The intensity of the revival had been too much for two already unstable and depressed men. The second of them, Joseph Hawley, was one of the most prominent citizens of Northampton, and also Jonathan's uncle. Jonathan tried to comfort the bereaved widow, and he worked hard to provide fatherly help to his two fatherless cousins. But it was to be one of these young men (Joseph Hawley Jr.) who would eventually take the leading role in the opposition to Jonathan.

Practically, the immediate result of the revival was an increased congregation. Work began on a new meeting house, next to the old one, in the summer of 1736. The spring thaw in March 1737 weakened the old structure, and one Sunday morning while Jonathan was preaching the entire gallery collapsed while full of people. Miraculously there were no fatalities. The new meeting house, with seating for 800, was used for the first time on 25 December 1737 (Edwards along with many Puritans did not celebrate Christmas Day). Huge debate was occasioned by the seating plan, which was arranged according to social standing. For a town that had supposedly experienced the grace of God in revival to exhaust so much nervous energy on a seating plan seems amazing, and their pastor told them so in no uncertain terms in the opening sermon.

But the revival was not over. From 1735 through to 1740 the rate of conversions slowed down considerably, but the mood of the town continued to be 'serious' and a good number of people met for prayer. The young people were more religiously minded than they had been for decades. The year 1740 marked the zenith of the dramatic revival movement throughout New England. Congregations began to experience outward excitement: people cried out with fear of damnation; others fainted; some wept. In the autumn of 1740 the English evangelist George Whitefield visited New England, and huge crowds gathered to hear him preach.

During 1741 the chief manifestation of revival in Northampton was the conversion of many of the children and young people in the town. By this time, Jonathan himself had became a sought-after preacher, and received many invitations outside his own church. One sermon, 'Sinners in the Hands of an Angry God', which he had preached to little outward effect at Northampton, resulted in scenes of mass hysteria in the church at nearby Enfield when he repeated it there in July 1741.

There were scenes of great excitement in Northampton in January 1742 when a young visiting preacher by the name of Samuel Buell came to supply the pulpit in Jonathan's absence. But this was the last year they were to experience revival.

The revival had caused bitter division among the ministers of New England: around a third of them dismissed it as merely human emotion and mass hysteria. Jonathan Edwards was realistic enough to understand this reaction. He agreed that a dramatic 'conversion experience' meant precisely nothing unless it was followed by a lifetime of obedience. It could be worse than useless, because the excitement of the 'experience' could lead individuals to believe that they were infallible. 'Revival' could overflow into fanaticism. Heightened excitement could lead people into actions that were misguided, while they claimed it was the guidance of the Holy Spirit. Uneducated people were thrilled by the notion that God would speak directly to them, and make claims that were ineffably silly. Newly converted individuals denounced mature leaders as lacking the Spirit.

And yet the presence of the false did not negate the presence of the true. The revival contained both good and bad. And when Jonathan set out to analyse the unusual scenes that had resulted from this phenomenon called 'revival' he had a case study right by him. For Sarah too had had an extraordinary experience. Indeed, when he returned from a preaching engagement early in 1742, the whole town was wondering whether she would even survive until his return. She had been prostrated physically with religious ecstasy; she had been so taken up with a sensation of the love of God that she had leaped for joy; she had sometimes been unable to stop talking, and at other times unable to speak.

Typically, Jonathan did not rush to conclusions one way or the other. He was willing to face the possibility it could be due to nervous instability. But he wanted to analyse what had happened. He asked Sarah to sit down and describe every detail. She gave him a precise account of her spiritual experience that had lasted for seventeen days from 19 January to 4 February 1742 (*extract 2*). It was, concluded Jonathan, the most intense, pure, unmixed and well-regulated of any he had seen. He went on to explain that the *long-term* effect in Sarah's life was remarkable. She was now entirely resigned to God. She had given over to God the choice of life or death, for herself and her loved ones. She let God choose comfort or pain. Jonathan lived with Sarah and he, of all people, would know if this was just a passing phase. It was not. He could testify to her continual peace, cheerfulness and joy in the coming months and years.

Jonathan was convinced of the reality of her experience. But it is at least possible that physical exhaustion and the nervous tension of her situation as pastor's wife left Sarah vulnerable to what we might call a breakdown or burn-out. In a less spiritual person this might have manifested itself simply in a stress-related illness, or nervous collapse. Sarah was, however, incredibly sensitive to spiritual influences, and the heightened religious excitement induced by Buell's visit to the town meant that her collapse took the form of a physical collapse accompanied by a genuinely ecstatic sense of the presence of God.

'A resignation of all to God' (1742–1758)

The reality of Sarah's 'resignation of all to God' would be tested all too soon.

While carried away with a sense of the love of God, she had visualized the worst-case scenarios that could befall her. What if the townsfolk turned on her and she was thrown out into the wilderness in the midst of winter? What if her husband turned against her? What if she had to die for Christ? More to the point, what about living the difficult day-to-day routine uncomplainingly? She was only thirty-two. She had already had seven children and there were four more confinements ahead, with all the pain, danger and exhaustion that involved.

If God loved her, Sarah could honestly say that she did not care about the rest.

But now she had to live through scenarios that she had not imagined: war, slander and intrigue, bereavement, poverty, a move to an isolated Indian settlement, continued poverty and continued intrigue and, finally, the loss of her beloved husband. How would she respond? This would be the ultimate test of her professed security in the love of God.

War

England and France went to war in 1744. Inhabitants of towns such as Northampton were immediately the targets of attack, because French Canadians were paying their allies among the Indians to kill English settlers. Daily reports circulated of gruesome killings. Both sides engaged in the revolting practice of paying bounties for the scalps of the enemy. In 1745 the Edwards' garden was chosen as the site of a watchtower from which the Northampton militia could guard against attack — at this point baby Eunice was two, and little Jonathan just a newborn. Several in Northampton were killed. This was not just a localized struggle: it was a global conflict between two naval powers. French Catholic victory, it was thought, would usher in a grim era of Protestants being burned at the stake. War was seen as divine judgement on a backsliding nation.

The war not only brought fear and insecurity, it led to financial chaos, the devaluing of currency and great economic hardship. The parishioners were all struggling. They found it hard enough to feed their own families, and the handing over of tithes for the Edwards' upkeep tended to go by the wayside. Jonathan and Sarah were in the embarrassing situation of having to remind the parish to pay their salary, and Jonathan (like other ministers of the time) was determined to get the salary arranged on a more regular basis. This did not go down well with his parishioners. Sarah faced the indignity of having to submit detailed and itemized accounts of all family expenditures to satisfy the townsfolk that they were not guilty of extravagance.

Slander and intrigue

The dispute over salary was symptomatic of the widening breach between Jonathan and the Northampton church. Relationships degenerated during the years after the end of revival in 1742, culminating in Jonathan's dismissal in 1750. The sense of rejection experienced by the family was stunning, and this was possibly the severest trial that Sarah had to bear. Jonathan had the gift of detachment — if his conscience was clear he was free from emotional turmoil. His farewell sermon to his people was a model of clear-sighted objectivity. He had been wronged, but there was no bitterness, and he was willing to wait for the final judgement for vindication. He continued to think, to write, and to correspond with friends in Scotland on profound theological issues. Yes, he was hurt, but he was a giant of a man, much bigger than what was going on in this little parish.

Sarah shared something of this; she was a kindred spirit and the wider interests of the kingdom of God were real to her too. But as a woman in a small, tightly-knit community she was only too aware of what people were thinking and saying. Were those looks and whispers hostile? Sympathetic? Pitying? Of necessity more exposed to the townspeople on a day-to-day level, she was more sensitive to currents of opinion. And she was powerless as a party came together who were absolutely determined to get rid of her husband. Leading members of this party were blood relatives. The ringleader was Joseph Hawley Jr., who would later confess that he had circulated vile slanders in an attempt to have his cousin dismissed. Feelings were electric. Certainly the

Edwards had a few stalwart friends whom they could trust. Chief among them was Jonathan's uncle, Colonel Stoddard, a pillar of the community, whose massive personality and reputation shielded them from some of the opposition. But Colonel Stoddard fell critically ill during a visit to New York in 1748. He asked Sarah to come down to nurse him in his final sickness — unhesitatingly she left her baby with a neighbour's wife, made arrangements for the family and went. His death left them all the more vulnerable.

But what was going on? Jonathan's ministry had seemed so successful during the years of growth from 1734 to 1742. Why this opposition?

Social and religious forces bigger than the local situation were at work. Revival had unleashed forces of individualism that were profoundly anti-authority. Church members were willing to question their pastor's judgement, and if he did not agree with them, why not dismiss him? After all, they too had experienced the Holy Spirit! Where there were party divisions, those who had experienced revival claimed divine support for their viewpoint.

The eighteenth century also saw a 'levelling' in American society. The old assumption that the minister (as a member of the gentry class) was entitled to a higher standard of living than the bulk of his parishioners came under attack. The Edwards were caught in the backlash. They believed that their 'station' necessitated a 'genteel' way of life. Jonathan, unlike the farmers around him, always wore his wig. There may have been a culture gap between the Edwards, who were well-educated and would have been far more at home in a city like Boston, and their farming neighbours. Jonathan was essentially an academic, albeit a kind and loving one! But he was seriously out of touch with the feelings of his parishioners.

Then too, as the eighteenth century progressed, the ideal of the community being identified with the church became outdated. Was the minister responsible for the morality of the town? In 1744 some of the young adults in the town were found joking over the illustrations in a midwifery handbook. A tragi-comic spectacle unfolded. From the pulpit Jonathan read out the names of all those involved, whether participants or witnesses. This was a huge mistake. All alike were shamed and angry, and they represented every important family in the town. Jonathan never recovered credibility after this.

The final cause of disagreement was a dispute over who should take communion. In an age of increasing 'democracy' to suggest *taking away* a long-held right was inflammatory. But this is what Jonathan, in effect, attempted to do. It was doomed.

His grandfather had allowed unconverted people to take communion. This was a sensitive issue, as only communicant members of the church could hold civic office in the town. By 1744 Jonathan had become convinced that only those who professed conversion should be admitted to church membership and allowed to take communion. But there was no way he was going to carry the church with him on this issue. Not only was he desecrating the memory of his revered grandfather, but he was challenging the cherished privileges of townsfolk. This issue stirred up tensions between 'nominal' church members (including some of Edwards' wider family) and the others.

In 1747 Joseph Hawley Jr. was elected to civic office in Northampton. He was young, dynamic, gifted, eloquent — and leading the opposition to Jonathan. In the following year, the death of Colonel Stoddard removed one of Jonathan's most loyal supporters. With him gone, the weight of influence in the extended family tipped over to Israel Williams, another cousin of Jonathan and one who had opposed him since 1734.

Jonathan's stand on the communion question provoked a furore, not only in Northampton, but also in the surrounding area. Ill-feeling was stirred up, and gross misrepresentations circulated, so much so that Sarah took up her pen in his defence, and described the way he had genuinely changed his mind over the years (*extract 3*). The church, however, dismissed Jonathan in June 1750, leaving the family with no means of financial support, and no immediate prospect of any alternative position.

And so, the scenario enacted in Sarah's imagination during her revival experience in essence, if not in detail, come to pass. In fact, to be literally thrown out might have been easier than the long months of living among unfriendly faces. The family did not move away from Northampton for a full year and four months after the dismissal. The level of hostility against Edwards and his family was devastating. In the small closed community they were the objects of scorn, and they could not escape.

There could have been no more effective test of Sarah's profession of love and humility. In the early days of 1742, while flat on her back, overwhelmed with awareness of God's love, she had been filled with an equally overwhelming love towards others. She could not even imagine bearing ill-will towards another person. She was so aware of her own sinfulness before God, and his free mercy to her, that she honestly reckoned that every other human being was more worthy than herself. And now she had some real-life enemies to deal with. Jesus said, 'Love your enemies.' Would she?

All the evidence is that she did. Jonathan and Sarah never spoke an unkind word about those who were circulating lies; they were transparently free of resentment or bitterness. Their own children bore witness to that. They conducted themselves with enormous dignity. They were shut up to the opinion of all but God. In later years Joseph Hawley Jr. wrote a grovelling letter of apology, admitting that his opposition had been sinful and wrong. Jonathan was content to accept a private apology, and wished Joseph the best. Neither he nor Sarah was interested in public vindication. Sarah's revival experience of humility and good-will to all had been proved genuine.

Bereavement

Sarah had felt able to submit whether *she* lived or died to God. Far more difficult for a mother is to submit the lives of her children. During this tense period Sarah experienced this trial for the first time.

In early 1747 David Brainerd, a young missionary to the native Americans, arrived at the Edwards' home suffering from tuberculosis. Sarah was pregnant with her tenth child, and her second daughter Jerusha volunteered to nurse him. It was not yet realized that tuberculosis (or consumption) is infectious. David died in October 1747; seventeen-year-old Jerusha followed him in February 1748. Death from tuberculosis is not pleasant. The strain of these horrible months was perhaps reflected in the fact that the child Sarah bore three months later was her only unhealthy baby (little Elizabeth suffered from rickets and was pitifully frail). But Jonathan and Sarah did not grieve hopelessly. They were convinced that Jerusha was with the Lord she loved. Once again their eternal perspective rescued them from self-pity or despair. Jerusha was in many ways 'the flower of the family', wrote Jonathan, and yet her parents had accepted that the Lord had given her — he could also take her away. The text chosen by her parents for the grave was Psalm 17:15: 'I shall be satisfied, when I awake, with thy likeness.'

This tragedy hit the whole family hard. Six years later, Esther wrote to her best friend Sarah Prince, 'We shall never forget the friends we have lost by death. I mean our *Sisters.*'[10]

Poverty

When Jonathan was dismissed from Northampton there was no severance package — his salary just stopped. He had a wife and ten children to provide for, and the bills still had to be paid.

Two months before Jonathan's dismissal Sarah gave birth to a son, their last child, who was given her maiden name, Pierrepont. Just two weeks before the dismissal her oldest child Sarah, aged twenty-one, married a faithful and loyal townsman, Elihu Parsons. These were glimmers of happiness amid the gloom. But the hard realities of life without an income soon began to take their toll. Friends in Scotland rallied around them with a generous collection, but this took time to arrive in New England. The strain told on Sarah, and she soon went down with rheumatic fever.

Sarah had been brought up in wealth and comfort, but she was willing to work hard. She had carefully trained her daughters in the art of needlework and fine embroidery, and they set to work to help the family finances. More expenditure was involved when another wedding took place in November 1750. Sarah's fourth daughter, sixteen-year-old Mary, married Timothy Dwight, their next-door neighbour in Northampton. By the time the family settled in Stockbridge, a missionary settlement on the frontier

Sarah Edwards (c.1750–1755)
by Joseph Badger, Yale University Art Gallery,
bequest of Eugene Phelps Edwards
© Reproduced with permission

about sixty miles from Northampton, they were heavily in debt.

Sarah engaged in every economy she could think of. Perhaps the most poignant is the way she sewed together every scrap of paper that could be retrieved — and it was on these patchwork pieces of waste paper that her husband wrote some of the greatest treatises ever produced in church history. It seems almost incongruous that Jonathan Edwards, the great theologian and philosopher, should end up as a missionary to native Americans in an obscure frontier settlement. The settlement numbered about twelve English families, and 150 native American families. The family moved to Stockbridge in October 1751. Here at least Jonathan was once again receiving a salary, and when they finally managed to sell the house in Northampton the financial situation eased.

Life on the frontier — and further danger from war (1752–1756)

Sarah had the task of settling her large family into a totally new situation. Probably there was enormous relief at finally getting out of Northampton. The move would have been hardest on nineteen-year-old Esther: sociable, witty and beautiful, she was ill-suited to the limited horizons of this primitive place. But there were some compensations. The natural beauty surrounding them was stunning, and winter provided wonderful opportunities for sport: sledging and skating. Lucy (fifteen), Timothy (thirteen), Susanna (eleven), Eunice (eight) and Jonathan Jr. (six) soon made friends among the children of the twelve English families (who had about forty children between them). Jonathan Jr. also made firm friends with numerous native American children and rapidly became bilingual. Little Elizabeth (four) was so fragile that she had to spend a lot of time indoors and there was often doubt as to whether she would survive another winter. Baby Pierrepont was oblivious to what was going on!

Jonathan set about his new duties among the native American Indians and the English settlers with characteristic resolve. Sadly, he and Sarah soon realized that tensions abounded even in that small settlement. Two leading English families (related to the Edwards) saw it as their mission to continue the Northampton opposition. Even here the Edwards could not shake off longstanding family enmity — here, too, there was continuing opportunity to 'love enemies'.

In the summer of 1752 Sarah, now aged forty-two, had the joy of seeing a third daughter happily married. Several young men had fallen helplessly in love with Esther, but she had not felt able to accept any proposals to date. When Aaron Burr, the thirty-six-year-old president of New Jersey College, visited Stockbridge in order to propose, Esther did not hesitate. This was a real love match despite the sixteen-year age gap. The family were happily unaware that this marriage would set in motion the series of tragedies soon to engulf them.

Aaron was snowed under with church and college commitments, and the Edwards family agreed that the wedding could take place down in New Jersey. Sarah travelled down with Esther for the marriage. Shortly afterwards she had to say goodbye to another of her children when fourteen-year-old Timothy was sent down to study at New Jersey College.

The family settled into some sort of routine in Stockbridge. Jonathan preached (via an interpreter) to the native Americans, and also preached to the small English congregation. He continued to write. Friendships were maintained, and Sarah still gave plenty of hospitality as old friends made the journey to see them even in this remote place. Their close friend Samuel Hopkins lived only seven miles away, and they always enjoyed his visits. Soon there was the excitement of the arrival of grandchildren. Their oldest daughter Sarah's first baby died. Sarah (junior) needed her family's support: she and her husband soon moved up to Stockbridge to be near the family. But after that they had healthy children, as did Mary and Esther. Sarah tried, if possible, to be at the birth of her grandchildren (family members commonly acted as midwives), and Jonathan had to resign himself to her absences. When Esther had her first child in the spring of 1754, Sarah travelled down to New Jersey to be with her.

That same year there were renewed threats from French-supported Huron Indians. In September, Hurons broke into the settlement one Sunday morning and killed and scalped three members of one English family. A fort was soon built around the Edwards' home. During the construction Sarah cooked 180 meals for the builders, in addition to 800 meals for refugees fleeing the interior.[11] When soldiers were sent to Stockbridge, Sarah was expected to feed them too. The budget simply could not stretch that far. Jonathan wrote to the officer in charge to say that they could not afford to supply more than four soldiers with provisions.

Friends and family begged the Edwards to leave Stockbridge, at least temporarily, as they were dangerously exposed to attack. But Jonathan and Sarah felt it was their duty to stay. They were safer in the path of duty than out of it. They feared God, not men. They bowed to prudence as far as to send the two smallest children down to stay with Mary and Timothy in Northampton in September 1754. Not all their children shared their calm faith. When Esther paid a surprise visit to her parents in September 1756 she could not sleep for fear, and confided to her friend Sally that she was simply unwilling to resign herself to being butchered in her bed. Her visit was all the more miserable because a few days after her arrival, Sarah left for Northampton to be with Mary during another confinement. It cannot have been easy for Sarah to leave Esther and her new grandchild Aaron, for she did not know when she would be able to see them again. But duty prevailed: the hazards of childbirth dictated that she should take her place with Mary.

In the midst of all this Jonathan continued to minister to the native American Indians in the immediate vicinity. He had a high regard for them, and the regard was mutual. 'The Indians seem much pleased with my family, especially my wife,' he wrote. His hope that his son Jonathan would eventually minister to the native Americans would, in time, be fulfilled. At age nine young Jonathan was already fluent in one American Indian language. His father then sent him to live with an English missionary in remote Onohquauga for two years to learn another.

'My God lives, and he has my heart' (1757–1758)

In 1757, Esther's husband died. She was heartbroken. Aaron had been the man of her dreams, and she unashamedly adored him. But this was only the catalyst for a series of tragedies to follow. Jonathan, now aged fifty-four, was invited to take Aaron Burr's place as President of the New

Jersey College. He moved down to Princeton to be with his widowed daughter, while Sarah finished packing their belongings in Stockbridge.

Shortly after he had taken up his new responsibilities a smallpox epidemic struck in 1758. Smallpox was one of the great scourges of the time. In previous centuries in Europe, it is estimated that in some years it caused a tenth of all deaths. Inoculation became more commonplace through the eighteenth century (inducing a mild dose of smallpox to produce immunity). The risks were minimal, compared with the risk of contracting the disease without being inoculated.[12] Almost as a routine, Jonathan was inoculated. It seemed at first that he would recover normally, but then he succumbed to fever and became critically ill. Some of his last words were to send love to his wife, thanking God for the 'uncommon union' that they had enjoyed — and would enjoy for eternity.[13] When Sarah received the terrible news of his untimely death she responded with a brief but unbearably poignant letter to Esther (*extract 4*). She had lost the one she loved more than any other: but she still loved the God who had given him — and taken him. 'The Lord has done it: He has made me adore his goodness that we had him so long. But my God lives and he has my heart.'

Esther never received the letter. She too died shortly afterwards, leaving two orphaned children. Sarah then had to leave her own children (little Pierrepont aged only eight) and travel down to New Jersey to collect her two orphaned grandchildren. Although she arrived in good health, she contracted dysentery and died after a short illness of just five days. She died peacefully, and expressed her total resignation of her life to God.[14] She was buried in her husband's grave. Sarah was aged just forty-eight when she died.

Four premature deaths within one year, and such gifted individuals! Aaron Burr, a dynamic preacher and college principal, and the extrovert, charming and affectionate Esther; Jonathan Edwards, the great writer and theologian, and the spiritually sensitive, warm and caring Sarah. A bleak and tragic conclusion to the story — and yet the influence of Jonathan and Sarah Edwards lives on.

Her character and significance

The so-called Great Awakening of the eighteenth century transformed the Protestant church, and laid the foundations for the modern mission movement. The revival took hold of people's emotions. Truth seemed to come alive. 'I feel my Saviour in my heart,' wrote the hymnwriter Charles Wesley (in the original verse 5 of 'And can it be?').[15] There were aberrations and excesses, as in any religious movement, but the greatest revival leader, Jonathan Edwards, certainly believed that his wife Sarah's intense and extraordinary spiritual experience represented the purest and highest elements in that revival period. It was experience solidly based on biblical truth, not divorced from it.

The description of Sarah's experience during the revival (*extract 2*) ranks alongside the most intense of mystical writings in any tradition. The description is firmly founded in Scripture and, most important of all, it stood the test of suffering. The reality of her enjoyment of God's love was severely tried, but she trusted God through difficult childbirths, the pain of rejection by the church she and Jonathan had served all their lives, the humiliation of intense poverty, bereavement, the dangers of war and the greatest pain of all in losing her husband at a premature age. Her serenity and poise in the face of these challenges demonstrated her unshakeable confidence that '... neither death nor life, neither angels nor demons, neither the present nor the future, nor any powers, neither height nor depth, nor anything else in all creation, will be able to separate us from the love of God that is in Christ Jesus our Lord (Romans 8:38–39).'

Of Sarah's children all except Jerusha and Elizabeth (who died aged fourteen) survived to adulthood — and lived useful, fulfilled lives. In 1900 a survey was made of Jonathan and Sarah's descendants. From this one marriage had come an astonishing array of people who had made useful contributions to society: clergymen, lawyers, professors, politicians, businessmen and doctors. One hundred missionaries had come from this single family. The author of the survey concluded that '...much of the capacity and talent, intensity and character of the more than 1,400 of the Edwards family is due to Mrs Edwards.'[16] The worst casualty of the deaths of Aaron and Esther was their son, Aaron Burr Jr. Inheriting his parents' brilliance, he was meteorically successful on one level (he became vice-president of the United States) but a disaster in emotional and moral terms. He was an exception: the vast majority of Jonathan and Sarah's descendants followed their example of integrity and service. And then there is the incalculable influence of the writings of Jonathan Edwards. As we have seen, humanly speaking, his capacity for such sustained work, often in such adverse circumstances, was largely due to Sarah's faithful support.

Selections from her writings

Extract 1: Jonathan's early description

This is not from Sarah's pen; it is the description Jonathan wrote of her when she was just thirteen:

They say there is a young lady in New Haven who is loved by that Great Being, who made and rules the world, and that there are certain seasons in which this Great Being, in some way or other invisible, comes to her and fills her mind with exceeding sweet delight; and that she hardly cares for anything except to meditate on him... She has a strange sweetness in her mind, and a singular purity in her affections, is most just and conscientious in her conduct, and you could not persuade her to do anything wrong or sinful if you would give her half the world, lest she should offend this Great Being. She is of a wonderful sweetness, calmness and universal benevolence of mind... She will sometimes go about from place to place, singing sweetly, and seems always to be full of joy and pleasure and no one knows for what. She loves to be alone, walking in the fields and groves, and seems to have someone invisible always conversing with her.[17]

Extract 2: Sarah's experience of 1742

Sarah herself described her experiences of January 1742, and her husband wrote down her account:

On Tuesday night, Jan. 19th, I felt very uneasy and unhappy at being so low in grace. I thought I very much needed help from God, and found a spirit of earnestness to seek help of him, that I might have more holiness. When I had for a time been earnestly wrestling with God for it, I felt within myself great quietness of spirit, unusual submission to God, and willingness to wait upon him, with respect to the time and manner in which he should help me...[18]

Her account continues with a description of how prayers, hymns, and the words of Scripture were all more meaningful to her than ever before: truths she had accepted before now lifted her into a kind of ecstasy. She was intensely aware of her own sin, of the love of the Father, of the presence of Christ, of the ministry of the Spirit. For example when the text in Romans 8, 'Who shall separate us from the love of God' was read:

I seemed to hear the great God proclaiming thus

*to the world concerning me; 'Who shall lay any-
thing to thy charge.' ... I cannot find language to
express how* certain *this appeared — the everlasting mountains and hills were but shadows to
it. My safety, and happiness, and eternal enjoyment of God's immutable love, seemed as durable
and unchanging as God himself... Under a
delightful sense of the immediate presence and
love of God, these words seemed to come over
and over again in my mind, 'My God, my all;
my God, my all.' The presence of God was so
near and so real, that I seemed scarcely conscious of anything else. God the Father and the
Lord Jesus, seemed as distinct persons, both
manifesting their inconceivable loveliness and
mildness and gentleness, and their great and
immutable love to me.*[19]

She wrote that the things she feared most: the ill will of
the town, or the disapproval of her husband, would now
mean nothing to her:

*My mind seemed as much above all such things,
as the sun is above the earth...*[20] *I awoke in the
morning of Thursday, Jan. 28th in the same
happy frame of mind, and engaged in the duties
of my family with a sweet consciousness that
God was present with me, and with earnest
longings of soul for the continuance and
increase of the blessed fruits of the Holy Spirit
in the town. About nine o'clock, these desires
became so exceedingly intense, when I saw
numbers of people coming into the house with*

an appearance of deep interest in religion, that my bodily strength was much weakened, and it was with difficulty that I could pursue my ordinary avocations. About 11 o'clock, as I accidentally went into the room where Mr Buell was conversing ... I felt such a sense of the ingratitude manifested by the children of God ... that my strength was immediately taken away, and I sunk down on the spot... Mr Buell then read a melting hymn of Dr Watts, concerning the loveliness of Christ ... my soul was drawn so powerfully towards Christ and heaven that I leapt unconsciously from my chair. I seemed to be drawn upwards, soul and body, from the earth towards heaven... At length my strength failed me, and I sunk down; when they took me up and laid me on the bed, where I lay for a considerable time, faint with joy, while contemplating the glories of the heavenly world. After I had lain a while, I felt more perfectly subdued and weaned from the world and more fully resigned to God than I had ever been conscious of before. I felt an entire indifference to the opinions and representations and conduct of mankind concerning me, and a perfect willingness that God should employ some other instrument than Mr Edwards in advancing the work of grace in Northampton. I was entirely swallowed up in God, as my only portion, and his honour and glory was the object of my supreme desire and delight. At the same time I felt a far greater love to the children of God than ever before... That night ... was the sweetest night I ever had

*in my life. I never before, for so long a time
together, enjoyed so much of the light, and rest
and sweetness of heaven in my soul, but without the least agitation of body during the whole
time... all night I continued in a constant, clear,
and lively sense of the heavenly sweetness of
Christ's excellent and transcendent love, of his
nearness to me, and of my dearness to him... I
seemed to myself to perceive a glow of divine
love come down from the heart of Christ in
heaven, into my heart, in a constant stream,
like a stream or pencil of sweet light. At the
same time my heart and soul all flowed out in
love to Christ, so that there seemed to be a
constant flowing and reflowing of heavenly and
divine love, from Christ's heart to mine; and I
appeared to myself to float or swim, in these
bright, sweet beams of the love of Christ,
like the motes swimming in the beams of the
sun... I think that what I felt each minute, during the continuance of the whole time, was
worth more than all the outward comfort and
pleasure which I had enjoyed in my whole life
put together... This lively sense of the beauty
and excellence of divine things continued
during the morning, accompanied with peculiar
sweetness and delight. To my own imagination,
my soul seemed to be gone out of me to God
and Christ in heaven, and to have very little
relation to my body. God and Christ were so
present to me, and so near me, that I seemed
removed from myself ... the glory of God
seemed to be all, and in all, and to swallow up*

every wish and desire of my heart ... when these words were read:

My sighs at length are turned to songs
The Comforter has come

so conscious was I of the joyful presence of the Holy Spirit, I could scarcely refrain from leaping with transports of joy...[21]

Her account goes on to describe another night in which she was awake most of the night 'with a constant delightful sense of God's great love and infinite condescension'; her soul remained in 'a kind of heavenly elysium'.[22] She became aware of an entire resignation to God's will: willing to die any death, and — even more of a test — willing to live for him. The next morning, on Sunday:

I felt a love to all mankind, wholly peculiar in its strength and sweetness, far beyond all that I had ever felt before... I never before felt so far from a disposition to judge and censure others... to do this seemed abhorrent to every feeling of my heart... The road between heaven and my soul seemed open and wide all the day long; and the consciousness I had of the reality and excellence of heavenly things was so clear, and the affections they excited so intense, that it overcame my strength, and kept my body weak and faint, the great part of the day, so that I could neither stand nor go without help...[23]

Extract 3: In defence of Jonathan

Jonathan's grandfather had permitted those to take communion who had not professed conversion. Jonathan came to the conviction that only those who had been converted should take communion. This provoked a furore, not only in Northampton, but also in the surrounding area. Ill feeling was stirred up, and gross misrepresentations circulated. In this letter, Sarah described the way he had genuinely changed his mind over the years.

I, the subscriber, do testify and declare that above four years ago, not very long after Mr. Edwards had admitted the last Person that ever was admitted into this church who made no Profession of Godliness, He told me that He would not dare ever to admit another Person without a Profession of real saving Religion; and the same Time told me he had put something into his Book on Religious Affections by which the Country would know his opinion, and that He had done it on Design that They might have some Intimation of it.

And not long after, when riding out with him, (I being ill, and riding for my Health) He had considerable discourse on this subject, and spake much of the great difficulties that He expected would come upon Him by reason of his opinion. I asked Him what Course he intended to take. He said he knew not what. I asked Him if He would not publish something expressly handling the subject & vindicating his opinion: He replied, not unless He was forced to it, for

He did [not] at all love openly to oppose his Grandfather in that manner: He said to preach against him would be looked upon as a great degree of arrogance (or to that purpose) and much more to print against Him. He chose rather for the present to content Himself with giving some occasional Intimations of his opinion, that People may be thinking of it; as (said He) I have already done in my Book on religious affections; when that Book comes out all my People will know that I am of that opinion, and added, I am still looking & inquiring into this matter and 'tis possible I may hereafter see otherwise.

He often touched on this matter in discourse with me before his Books on religious Affections came out; But when these Books came abroad He said to me that He wondered that He heard nothing of the People's taking notice that He differed from Mr. Stoddard. He very often said that He did think it probable that the People would never yield to his opinion; but yet from Time to Time expressed a full determination not to go on in admitting members without a credible Profession of Godliness any more, unless He should receive other Light, and often signified that when He should begin to have Occasion to act on his Principles, or when any offered to come into the Church, that made no pretense to Godliness, & He should be obliged to refuse, then the Tumult would begin.

And sometimes when we talked of the Probability of Col. Stoddard's disliking my opposing*

* The original MS reads 'my' but it would appear to be a mistake for 'his'.

the opinion & Practice of his Father, He always said to that Purpose that let that be as it would, it was his full determination to go on no longer as He had done, unless He had conviction offered. I several Times heard Mr. Edwards say that He thought it his best way to improve his Time in endeavoring to get Light, 'till He was obliged to act, and that He chose to give some intimations of his opinion before He had occasion to act, lest when He came to refuse any one that offered Himself to join with the church, giving as a Reason of it that He had changed his opinion, It should be suspected that this was not the True Reason, but that this Refusal was indeed from personal Prejudice.

I often heard Mr. Edwards speak freely of his forementioned opinion, and his Resolution to proceed no further &c, before his Family & before others, both Town People and Strangers, before Col. Stoddard's death, & before his salary was settled, and never as a secret Thing or a Thing that He desired would be kept so; nor had I ever any Imagination that He desired it should be kept secret; and therefore both I & my children often freely spoke of it when we had Occasion. I often heard Mr. Edwards speak of these Things to Mr. John Brainerd; and particularly of the Probability of its ending in a separation between Him and his People.

I heard him once speak of these Things very freely and fully about four years ago, when Mr. Buel & Mr. Osborn of Long Island & Lieut. Phelps & Mr. Noah Parsons of this Town were present; & while he was discoursing of it, Noah Lyman came in & Mr. Edwards did not at all forbear on that account but still went on freely uttering the same things. I remember He once talked of it to Col. Dwight before his salary was settled, who never had I Suppose, at that Time Intimated any favourable Thought of his opinion. He once before Col. Stoddard's death talked largely of the matter in my hearing with Mr. Burr of Newwark, Mr. Strong, now settled at Portsmouth, being present. He told Mr. Burr that He should be glad to see otherwise if He could, for as his judgment now was, He could proceed no further in our Former way; tho' it was not unlikely that his Refusal might be a means of Throwing him out of Business, & bringing Him & his Family to Poverty. Mr. Burr then said to Him 'If the case be so, you had better run away from these difficulties and accept the Place of the President of N-Jersey College.' Mr. Edwards replied He must not run away before He was called, for these difficulties were not come upon Him yet.

I remember Mr. Edwards once in talking to some Gentleman of these matters Expressed Himself thus, that the difficulties He had a Prospect of appeared to Him like a Bottomless ocean, He could see no end of 'em. I once asked Him whether it was worth his while to strive to have his salary settled seeing He thought it probable that this difficulty would end in a separation between Him & his People; He answered, there were so great difficulties, arose through the

*salaries being unsettled that if he tarried but a
year or two longer He chose to have it done. I
can further testify that to my observation, Mr.
Edwards's being of this opinion was publicly
talked of abroad, three years ago the last
February, and that I then heard it openly talked
of at Hartford & New Haven, & being enquired
of about it there, spoke of it freely myself. I also
once talked freely of it to Elisha Pomeroy going
to Boston with Him before Col. Stoddard's death.*

*Northampton, June 17th. 1750
SARAH EDWARDS*[24]

Extract 4: Letter to Esther Burr

When Sarah heard of her husband's death (which took
place on 22 March 1758) she was in poor health herself.
She had just been preparing for a visit to her widowed
mother-in-law (Jonathan Edwards' father having died on
27 January, a couple of months before his son). Crippled
with pain in her neck, she managed to write these few
lines to Esther; they transparently convey her 'resignation
of all to God':

Stockbridge, April 3rd, 1758.

*My very dear child,
What shall I say? A holy and good God has
covered us with a dark cloud. O that we may
kiss the rod, and lay our hands on our mouths!
The Lord has done it. He has made me adore his
goodness that we had him [her husband] so long.*

But my God lives; and he has my heart. O what a legacy my husband and your father has left us! We are all given to God; and there I am, and love to be.

Your ever affectionate mother,
Sarah Edwards. [25]

ANNE
STEELE

1717–1778

Birthplace of Anne Steele, Broughton

Key dates & places

1717 Birth of Anne Steele

1720 Mother died

1723 Father remarried

1732 Baptized by immersion aged fifteen

1737 Suitor drowned

1739 Father became pastor of Broughton Chapel

1742 Declined proposal of marriage from Benjamin Beddome

1760 Two-volume set of Anne's hymns and poems published

1778 Death of Anne

England

London

Bath

Broughton

Salisbury

*A*nne Steele lived during the eighteenth century in a small village in the south-west of England. Part of a well-off and closely-knit family, she deliberately remained single in an age that assumed that the ideal for women was marriage and motherhood. Through correspondence, she participated in a lively circle of educated and witty friends. Two volumes of her hymns and poems were published during her lifetime. Anne suffered ill health for much of her life (modern doctors reckon she had a persistent form of malaria). Despite this, she was a cheerful woman, whose faith (and sense of humour) kept her positive even through times of intense pain.

The setting

Eighteenth-century England was a place of extremes: huge and ostentatious country palaces for the aristocracy at the top of the social pyramid, gross filth and poverty for the poor of town and country alike. In between there were families such as the Steeles: wealthy, comfortable and secure. Their experience was worlds away from either the gross opulence of the few, or the dire poverty of the many.

But the Steeles' economic well-being was only one side of the story. They, along with other Dissenters, were regarded as second-class citizens, because they would not join the state church. Although the 'Glorious Revolution' of 1688 had secured freedom to worship for Nonconformists they were still excluded from the universities and from civic and political life. Unable to enter the majority of professions, many Dissenters devoted themselves to business and trade — often very successfully. When Anne's father and brother engaged in business deals worth tens of thousands of pounds, they were applying to the timber trade the ability that — had they been Anglicans — would probably have been used in Parliament or law. The Dissenters even turned their exclusion from the ancient universities to their advantage, setting up academies that (unfettered by ancient tradition) became centres of excellence.

Such toleration as the Dissenters had was fragile. Queen Anne (reigned 1702–1714) and her High Church advisers loathed them. Meetinghouses were sometimes burned down by Tory mobs. Prospects brightened when Queen Anne died. She left no living children, and the throne went to George, Elector of Hanover (a little state in modern-day Germany). Anne Steele lived through the reigns of two of the Georges (George I, reigned 1714–1727; George II, reigned 1727–1760) and into the reign of the third (the 'mad' King George III, reigned 1760–1820). During this 'Hanoverian' dynasty, Dissenters worshipped freely, but still suffered discrimination in the areas of higher education and employment.

If Nonconformists found their options limited in the eighteenth century, women were even more restricted. They were barred from just about everything except marriage. But England was increasingly a literate society, and some women in this century found fulfilment in writing. Anne was one of these. She was fortunate to belong to a family prosperous enough to educate her and willing to support her. The eighteenth century saw a massive increase in reading among both sexes. Newspapers found avid readers from all classes, poetry was enormously popular and, from the mid-century, romantic novels became increasingly fashionable.

Culturally, the eighteenth century saw the beginning of the Romantic Movement. Conventional religion seemed unattractive, but many found solace in contemplation of the beauties of nature. It became popular to repudiate the mannered and artificial, in favour of the natural and spontaneous. Rural life was praised; there was a retreat into sentiment and 'sensibility'. Certainly the full flowering of these tendencies came later (e.g. the poems of William Wordsworth, 1770–1850), but we see in the poems of Anne Steele some typical themes: the love of early evening as a time of reflection and solitary peace, the love of nature, and what Kenneth Clarke described as the 'gentle melancholy'[1] characteristic of this movement. The poet William Cowper (1731–1800) was a near contemporary of Anne, and his poetry sometimes strikes a similar note: 'God made the country, and man made the town.'[2]

This century was not a time of unbroken peace. In particular, Jacobite rebels attempted to place the Catholic 'James III' on the throne in 1715, and again in 1745. They did not succeed, but there was real fear of civil war. Twenty-eight-year-old Anne wrote home during a trip away in 1745 to say that she could not sleep peacefully — she was so terrified of possible invasion.[3] She and her family, like all Dissenters, knew that if the Jacobites installed a Catholic monarch, their liberties would be removed.

There was also the fear of Catholic conquest from outside. Special prayer meetings were called at Broughton — and many other places — during the conflict between the two great naval powers of Protestant England and Catholic France. War broke out in 1744, and rumbled on intermittently for the rest of the century in North America, the West Indies, India and Europe. Even in a quiet village like Broughton the battles were followed with excitement and apprehension. Anne composed several poems and hymns marking national events. She saw the war as a sign of God's just wrath, and every English victory as a token of his mercy.

The story

Anne's family and church background

Broughton is a small, peaceful village in the south of England, twelve miles east of Salisbury, and twelve miles west of Winchester. The Steeles were one of the more prosperous families in the community. They had been, for years, the leading family in the Particular Baptist Chapel,[4] which was one of the most ancient in the country.

In 1653, 111 Christians had first met together to found a Baptist chapel in Broughton and Porton. These were the days of 'heroic Dissent' — there was a price to pay for Nonconformity. Nine of them were baptized at the first meeting — an act of courage, as believer's baptism was still illegal. The work survived vicious years of persecution from 1660 to 1688. By the end of the eighteenth century the church was sending preachers out to other areas, and at one time had three ordained ministers and several preaching elders as well. Meetings were held at both sites until 1690 when it was decided to settle at Broughton.[5] Nine years later, in 1699, Henry Steele became pastor.

He had already been a member for nineteen years and had engaged in itinerant preaching. Henry remained the pastor at Broughton for the next forty years until his death in 1739. He did not take any financial support from the church, as he had made a fortune in contracting timber for the British Navy.

Henry had no son: his nephew William (Anne's father) assisted him in his business and in the preaching. William ended up taking over both the business and the pastorate in 1739. The family home was an elegant and spacious building called 'Grandfathers', with fine furniture and pictures and beautiful gardens. Here William and his first wife Anne rejoiced at the birth of a son and daughter, named after themselves (William, born in 1715, and Anne, born in 1717). Sadly, when another baby arrived in 1720, both mother and infant died.

William was left alone to care for five-year-old William and three-year-old Anne. Three years later he remarried — another Anne. His second wife, like his first, came from a prosperous Particular Baptist family. In keeping with the Puritan tradition, she kept a journal.[6] The entries give much valuable insight into the life of Anne Steele — they also show her stepmother, Anne Cater Steele, to be a woman of strong religious feeling. She took her responsibility for her stepchildren William and Anne (nicknamed Nany or Nanny) very seriously. She tried hard not to favour her own child, Mary (nicknamed Molly), born a year after her marriage. She agonized and prayed when Anne and Molly quarrelled. She prayed earnestly for the spiritual welfare of each child. She worried about sending them away to boarding school; she fretted over the 'secular' books that they enjoyed. Each time they left home — whether on a day trip to Weyhill Fair or for longer visits to relatives or friends, she prayed earnestly that they would be kept from sin. She was overjoyed when they professed conversion and were baptized. Mrs Steele was a worrier, and probably irritated her family immensely at times, but she and Anne became close companions, especially after William and Molly left home. Her diary records times of 'sweet' or 'delightful' conversation about spiritual things with Anne.

Chapel life

Life for the Steele children revolved around the regular meetings of the Baptist chapel.[7] While William, Anne and Molly were small, they were accustomed to hearing their great-uncle Henry preach. Services on Sunday mornings and afternoons were simple: extemporaneous prayers offered by the minister, metrical psalms and hymns 'lined out'[8] by one of the congregation and the sermon. Sometimes there were meetings for informal discussion on Sunday evenings, and there was at least one mid-week prayer meeting, often including a lecture. Notes from these lectures were printed and circulated. Baptisms were conducted in the baptistery, which had been constructed by 1727 (the person who filled it received payment of one shilling). Baptismal candidates wore special clothes: probably a long black robe for the men and a plain white long dress for the women. The Lord's Supper was celebrated once a month preceded by serious preparation, both corporate and individual. The table was 'closed' — that is, only baptized believers in membership of that church or another recognized fellowship could participate. New members would be welcomed into the fellowship at the Lord's Supper following their baptism. Membership was a serious business:

attendance at the meetings was expected, but also adherence to the covenant, which committed members to pray for and mutually support one another. Non-attendance or obvious 'sin' was punished at first with suspension from the Lord's Supper, and, if there was no repentance, excommunication.

Membership at the chapel stood at around fifty-one when Anne was fourteen. The next year, she and her brother William both gave their testimony to the church meeting, and were baptized — along with nine others. Most of these were the children or servants of already existing members. It was customary in the eighteenth century for applicants for baptism and church membership to give an extemporary verbal account of their conversion. Baptists cherished the 'gathered church' principle — that only truly converted people were members. While they looked anxiously for 'signs' of conversion in their young children, who often professed faith, it was common to wait at least until mid-teens before youngsters 'gave in their experience'. This was virtually the only time that females could speak in the church meeting — after this, unless they were asked a question, they were expected to be silent. It seems that often people found the 'giving in of their testimony' an unnerving experience, and many churches softened the demand during the following century, allowing them to submit a written testimony or else relying on a membership interview with at least two senior members or church office holders.

Anne's education

Anne was an affectionate, sensitive child, who was very close to her elder brother, William. Home life was happy, but educational opportunities were limited. Thus, as was common among more prosperous families, the Steele children were sent to boarding school.[9] There was a Dissenting Academy at nearby Trowbridge. Anne was sent to a boarding school which was probably a sister school for girls linked to this academy. We have one letter written from school in September 1729 when Anne was twelve. It was addressed to her stepmother. Anne had heard of the death of her aunt, and says that she hopes her young cousins will submit patiently to the providence of God. She writes that the main part of her education at that point is sewing 'headcloths'. This must have been frustrating, to say the least, for such an active mind. And, she also comments dryly, her schoolmistress is an 'odd-tempered woman'! (*extract 1*).

We do not know how long Anne stayed at this school. Two years later, when Anne was fourteen, we find the first of very many references in Mrs Steele's diary to 'the ague' — Anne and Molly suffered intermittently from it, and a modern doctor has argued convincingly that they probably suffered from recurring malaria.[10] This was common in England at the time, and was especially associated with marshy, low-lying areas. 'Grandfathers' was near the water meadows of Wallop. 'Chronic malaria would have had a progressively debilitating effect on Anne, the major consequences of which would have been anaemia, weakness, and susceptibility to other infections.'[11] It also caused fits associated with high fever, and left Anne vulnerable to consumption. For the rest of her life, Anne never enjoyed any sustained periods of good health, and she was often in great pain. She seems to have also suffered from terrible stomach pain (probably peptic ulcer disease), and from agonizing toothache (common in a century when dental hygiene was primitive and the treatment barbaric).[12] From now on her health would be a constant worry, and there are many anguished references to this in Mrs Steele's diary. She was told that Anne probably had consumption and she often feared that Anne might die.

In April 1733, Mrs Steele sent Anne (aged sixteen) and Molly (aged nine) to boarding school in Salisbury. Many in the chapel feared that the girls would be dangerously exposed to worldly influences. Mrs Steele agonized long and hard over the decision to send them. In June she had a visit from the elderly pastor, Henry Steele, who rebuked her for the sin of sending her girls away to school. 'I defended myself as well as I could in such a doubtful case [she wrote] but my thoughts were pretty much ruffled about it.'[13]

The relationship between Anne and her sister Molly could be stormy. In a letter to her older brother, Anne refers to Molly's ill temper. In 1734, when Anne was seventeen and Molly ten, Mrs Steele wrote in her diary of the 'feuds' between them. She sensed that this might be partly because she was partial to her own daughter, and prayed for grace to treat them equally.

Apart from school, William, Anne and Molly also made various visits to friends and relatives. In the summer of 1734 they stayed with their cousins at Haycombe, near Bath. Anne wrote from there on 27 September 1734, assuring her stepmother that Molly was well and happy (*extract 2*). Her letter shows her to be affectionate — she loves being with her relations, but also longs to be home with her parents.

In the autumn of the same year Anne visited Whitchurch for three weeks. Mrs Steele always prayed fervently for protection when her children went off on their trips, and with good reason. Roads were terrible (in the north it was not unknown for people to drown in the pot holes) and frequented by armed highwaymen. Heavy rain in summer could make roads just as impassable as they regularly were in winter. Nasty injuries often resulted when people were thrown from their horses. When Anne was eighteen, her father was on his way to a preaching engagement in the next village when his horse threw him and then trod on his right leg. But it was his other leg that was horribly fractured, with 'bones and marrow coming through the skin', as his wife recorded graphically in her diary. He could not move out of bed for five weeks. But her father survived the necessary operation to set the leg (no anaesthetics then!) and lived to be seventy-nine, albeit with one leg a good inch shorter than the other! The same summer we know that Anne was thrown from her horse and hurt her hip. (As there is no further mention of this incident it certainly did not leave her a lifelong invalid as some writers have inferred.)[14]

While we have no firm knowledge of the content of Anne's formal education, it seems likely that the ongoing education provided by communication and correspondence with her family's circle of friends was just as important. A typical social evening involved conversation on a wide variety of topics, and sometimes the reading of poetry and other literature (*extract 3*). Anne and her friends encouraged each other in their own creative efforts as well.

Singleness: a conscious choice

From Salisbury, Anne and Molly moved to Ringwood. They had friends there, the Manfields, and Molly continued her schooling, supervised by Anne. By the time Anne was twenty she had commenced a courtship with a young man named Mr Elcomb. We know little of him, except that he was well respected and generally liked in his community. When he drowned in a bathing accident, James Manfield immediately sent a messenger from Ringwood to tell the Steeles of the tragedy. He wanted them to know straight away, because he was not sure 'how far he [Elcomb] may have prevailed in the affections of Miss Steele'. He went on to explain that Elcomb had gone to the river to wash, went out of his depth and was swept away by the current.[15]

The Baptist historian Joseph Ivimey (1830) romantically wrote that this tragedy happened the day before the wedding of Anne and Elcomb. It then became popular to think that Anne's nerves never recovered (and that the hymn 'Father whate'er of earthly bliss'[16] was her response to the tragedy). But in the light of Manfield's letter it is inconceivable that the wedding was the next day — or even that a firm date had been set. Moreover there is no evidence, either in Anne's subsequent writings or in the diaries of her stepmother, to indicate that Anne suffered from a perpetually broken heart.

We have some letters which Anne wrote from Ringwood two years or so after the accident, written in a light-hearted and relaxed tone. She (in her early twenties) was acting as chaperone and teacher to Molly (in her mid-teens). She informed their stepmother that Molly was making young friends, and that her dancing lessons were going well. She mentioned that the clothes that she and Molly had with them were not nearly fashionable enough for the company at Ringwood, and gently suggested purchasing some new ones.

In 1739, when Anne was twenty-two, her great-uncle Henry died. He had been pastor for forty years. Her father, William, had been assisting him and preaching regularly for many years, and he now took over the pastorate. The chapel was enjoying a time of growth. Just eight years later, in 1745, the membership peaked at ninety-one. There had been many baptisms (thirty-seven in the period from 1730–1739) but after 1745 things began to decline, and in the following decade there were only four baptisms recorded. Things looked up a bit after that, and from 1759–1768 there were twelve new members, all but one coming in through confession of faith and baptism. These modest numbers were in contrast to the dramatic scenes of mass religious excitement provoked elsewhere by revival preachers such as John Wesley (1703–1791) and George Whitefield (1714–1770). But the chapel taught the necessity of personal conversion, which was the same basic message as that of the revival preachers; Anne's parents did on occasion go to hear Whitefield preach, and Methodist itinerant preachers were welcomed at the chapel.

Anne's father William was a successful businessman, and he continued to support himself through the timber trade. But he also became a devoted pastor. His second wife threw herself into the life of the church (she took an active part in working with the women — speaking with them about spiritual matters and advising about baptism). His children were also keen members. Anne's sensitivity to the needs of public worship inspired her to write hymns on the whole range of themes appropriate to different occasions and to fit the range of topics covered in the preaching ministry (*extracts 4,5,6*).

When Anne was twenty-five, she received a proposal of marriage from the minister of the Particular Baptist Chapel at Bourton-on-the-Water, Benjamin Beddome. He too was twenty-five, and he poured out his heart in a passionate (if ungrammatical) proposal:

Dear Miss,
Pardon the Boldness which prompts me to lay
these few lines at your Feet. If continued thoughts
of you ... may be considered as Arguments of
Love, surely I experience the Passion. If the
greatness of a Persons love will make up for the
Want of Wit, Wealth & Beauty, then may I
humbly lay claim to your Favour. Since I had the
happiness of seeing you How often have I
thought of Milton's beautiful Description of Eve,
Book 8 Line 471,

                              ... So lovely fair!
That what seem'd fair in all the World seem'd now;
Mean, or in her summ'd up, in her contain'd,
And in her Looks, which from that time infused
Sweetness into my Heart, unfelt before...

Mad'm give me leave to tell You that these
Words speak the very Experience of my Soul,
nor do I find it possible to forbear loving You?
Would You but suffer me to come and lay
before You those Dictates of a confused Mind
which cannot be represented by a trembling
Hand & Pen. Would You but permit me to cast
my self at your Feet & tell you how much I love,
Oh What an easement might you thereby afford
to a burdened Spirit, at the same time give me
an opportunity of declaring more fully that I
am in Sincerity
Your devoted Serv't
Benj. Beddome[17]

Dear Miss

Pardon the Boldness which prompts me to lay these few lines at your Feet. If continued Thoughts of you & a dislike to every thing besides may be considered as Arguments of Love surely I experience the Passion. & if the greatness of a Persons love will make up for the Want of Wit, Wealth & Beauty, then may I humbly lay claim to your Favour. — Since I had the happiness of seeing you How often have I thought of Milton's beautifull Description of Eve Book 8 Line 471

So lovely fair!
That what seemd fair in all the World seemd now;
Mean, or in her summd up, in her contain'd,
And in her Looks; which from that time infus'd
Sweetness into my Heart, unfelt before.

Madm give me leave to tell You that these Words speak the very Experience of my Soul, nor do I find it possible to forbear loving You. Would You but suffer me to come & lay before You these dictates of a confused Mind which cannot be represented by a trembling Hand & Pen. Would You but permit me to cast my self at your Feet & tell You how much I love, Oh What an easement might you thereby afford to a burdend Spirit, & at the same time give me an opportunity of declaring more fully that I am in Sincerity Your devoted Servt

Benjn Beddome

Benjamin Beddome's proposal of marriage to Anne Steele, written from Bourton on 23 December 1742. This letter is held in the Steele Collection at the Angus Library, Regents College, Oxford.
© *Reproduced with permisson*

We have no record of Anne's reply. It seems that Beddome's eloquence failed to persuade her. Beddome evidently recovered sufficiently from his disappointment to marry Elizabeth Bothwell at a later date.

In 1749, at the age of twenty-five, her half-sister Molly (now known as Mary) married Joseph Wakeford and moved to Andover. Notwithstanding the 'feuds' of their youth, Anne and Mary maintained a warm friendship for the rest of their lives. Anne often went to stay with the Wakefords in Andover, and they kept up a lively correspondence. They used classical pseudonyms when writing to each other: Anne was 'Sylviana', and Mary was 'Amira'.

Mary's letters to Anne hint at the restrictions and frustrations of family life. When her husband is away she nearly goes insane with the limitations of 'baby talk' all day. When unexpected visitors arrive she panics because the house is in disorder. She finds that her husband is not as ready to converse about spiritual things as members of the Steele family had been. She is so distracted with household concerns that she cannot get two thoughts in a straight line to write in an intelligent way to Anne. Despite all this, she often tried to persuade Anne to marry. A typical exchange between them in verse gives Anne's view of marriage — perpetual worry about one's spouse; and Mary's view of singleness — the dangers of falling in love with unsuitable men, and the fears of losing one's looks. Anne's settled view was that '...wives give up their freedom in one fatal day' (*extract 7*).

When Anne later told Mary that she had refused another marriage proposal, Mary gave her a good telling off. Anne coolly replied that she was happy as she was, and marriage brings with it many thorns. Indeed when she looked into the 'meadow' of marriage it was usually winter! Mary responded that everyone else puts up with the thorns, so why should Anne not do the same? Besides, most people find that flowers grow on the thorns — although she had to admit there were not many on hers at the moment! Mary admits too that many women marry (even though they might be better off on their own) just for the sake of custom — why does Anne not conform to custom like everyone else? This sample of light-hearted banter between the sisters dispels the notion that Anne suffered a bruised and broken heart all her life (*extracts 8,9*).

Anne remained single. She was in many ways privileged. She enjoyed financial independence; she had a comfortable home, a warm family circle and the freedom to visit friends. In her many sicknesses, her stepmother proved to be a devoted nurse. Anne had the time and opportunity to write. Her father had fixed an elegant room for her with the latest shelving and a fireplace. She enjoyed constant visits to the large and elegant home built near to 'Grandfathers' by her brother William. His home had a beautiful terrace and a walkway, lined with fir trees, where Anne wrote some of her verse. It is unsurprising, then, that she described her lifestyle as 'a fine even path' (final letter in *extract 8*), and that she hesitated to exchange it. At the age of thirty-three she wrote to her sister-in-law Mary (who was away on a visit):

> ... *Broughton is now pleasant and I only want my mother and you here and sister Molly well to make it quite agreeable. The rural scenes are in their perfection, how would you be delighted with a walk in your Garden, 'tis now in its finest dress, 'tis pity the Flowers would not stay till your return; but those little emblems of earthly*

*pleasure will soon wither and be no more. My
Cell too has its charms, the honeysuckle at my
Window is in full bloom, and I am sometimes
entertained with the soft warbling of a neigh-
bouring nightingale...*[18]

So Anne chose to remain at home with her father and
stepmother. The three of them often dined with her brother
and his wife and they regularly entertained visitors, many
of them from their circle of Particular Baptist friends and
relatives. Conversation was lively and wide-ranging.
Friendships were maintained and cultivated by means of
correspondence. Letters went far beyond narrow, personal
concerns. They included discussions of wider issues, spiritual
matters, poetry, and were sometimes written in a formal
'high style' that makes them mini-works of literature. Anne
was by no means frustrated in her singleness — her gifts
of writing blossomed in a way that might not have been
possible had she succumbed to Benjamin Beddome's
fervent plea, and become a busy pastor's wife. Moreover
her indifferent health would probably have collapsed
altogether under the rigours of pregnancy and child-rearing.

Rural tranquillity: the preferred option

Anne was born, lived and died in Broughton. Her life was
relatively uneventful, but not uninteresting. One of her light-
hearted poems paints a vivid picture of a typical winter
evening: animated conversation and extempore rhyming
games round the fire on a cold winter night (*extract 3*).
Anne was acutely aware of the privileged life she led,
compared with those around who lived in poverty. At the
age of thirty-four she wrote:

I often reflect with pleasure on the kindness of Providence in the many personal and relative blessings I enjoy and wish for a more lively sense of gratitude to the Almighty Donor — I look around me and see everywhere objects of pity, and while many of my neighbours complain of sickness, poverty and distress, I and mine are indulged with ease and plenty, why are we thus favoured? how can we enough acknowledge the distinguishing goodness which thus regards us?[19]

Anne found the quietness of village life exactly conducive to what she enjoyed most: the pleasures of the mind — thinking, praying and writing (*extract 10*). Not that she was anti-social. As health permitted, she engaged in mercy ministries to the poor. Moreover, much of her writing took the form of correspondence with a cultured and witty circle of friends, mainly men, many of them ministers: John Lavington (1690–1759) from the Exeter Baptist Chapel; Philip Furneaux (1726–1783) from London; James Fanch (1704–1767) from Romsey; Caleb Evans (1737–1791) of Bristol and John Ash, minister of the Baptist chapel at Pershore (c.1724–1779).[20] Furneaux helped get her work published in 1760, and Evans and Ash collaborated on a further edition of her poems after her death.

Anne loved the countryside. For example, in a letter to her sister Mary she contrasts the noise and bustle of fashionable town life with the tranquillity of her life in Broughton:

... I think I have heretofore found as much pleasure scribbling in my lonely retirement as a

fine Lady could do at a Ball, glittering among a crowd of Belles and Beaus. — poor comparison — 'Tis true I can have no notion of the high delight those gay flutterers taste, but as I imagine they are generally strangers to serious reflection, I think their entertainments deserve not to be named with the pleasure enjoy'd by a contemplative mind.[21]

Anne's appreciation of 'retirement' from fashionable society is also evident in a letter to her sister-in-law. She remarks that the exquisite and unaffected clothing of the flowers all around her is finer by far than the fashionable dress of the belles and beaus in town, and the artless music of the birds so much more charming than the music of the drawing room.[22] She is undoubtedly sincere, but her rhapsodic descriptions of the charms of nature, and her unfavourable comparison of high society with the 'natural' and 'rural' delights of village life, are typical of the writing of the Romantic Movement. For example, Thomas Gray (1716–1771, author of poems such as 'Elegy Written in a Country Churchyard') and William Collins (1721–1759, author of poems such as 'To Evening') were contemporaries. Anne and her friends took the rhetoric of the Romantic Movement further than some others, in that 'retirement' was seen as facilitating worship to the Creator. Many of her poems and hymns capture Anne's sense of the presence of God as she enjoyed the beauties of nature.

Anne's spirituality

Our main source for information about Anne's life is her stepmother's journal. It provides valuable insight into her everyday life but not as much as we would like concerning her spiritual life. From the few letters we have, and from her hymns (*extracts 4–6,11–12*), we can see that Anne's life was characterized by a consistent gratitude for God's goodness, a steady desire to experience his presence and a realistic sense of the temporary nature of earthly things.

The following letter was written to her brother William from Trowbridge when she was nineteen. We can see her serious attitude, her somewhat introspective anxiety that she be found in a correct 'frame' (conscious enjoyment and awareness of the presence of God), her awareness that every thought and action is seen by God and her eagerness for her brother to write and encourage her spiritually:

I really believe your writing to me would be very useful, both to improve my understanding, and to exalt my thoughts more to the solid pleasures of virtue and religion; the most necessary and important subjects. What are all the amusements of sense, to the divine contemplations of eternal things? They are empty and unsatisfying in their nature and short in duration, but these lift the thoughts to Heaven, and fill the soul with the most refined and lasting joy! But alas my mind is covered with a senseless stupidity: the continual din of a noisy town seems to dull my senses, and turn my thoughts all into confusion. O how desirable is the quiet enjoyment of the solitary fields! where no clamorous noise, or hurry, torments the ear, or disturbs the sight but the eyes and thoughts are at liberty to contemplate the wonders of creation in all their blooming pride and native beauty. But ah, why do I blame the change of place; when the chief fault is in myself: for though noise and company may sometimes take up the thoughts, yet 'tis my own carelessness which sinks me into such a dead inactive frame; and dulls the nobler faculties of my soul. Could we consider as we ought the all-seeing eye of God which surveys the inmost recesses of the heart, and marks every wandering thought; and have our minds filled with a religious awe of his divine presence: it would certainly make us more tender & careful of offending him by our sinful frames who cannot endure sin in his sight, and who hates all the workers of iniquity — how miserable then are we, our hearts are depraved with sin, and we have lost the original purity of our first creation; and are utterly incapable of ourselves of doing anything acceptable in the sight of God, but must acknowledge our impotence and fly to the blood of a Redeemer: where alone relief is to be found. If you'll please write to me, I hope it may be useful (by the blessing of God) to stir me to a more active and vigorous frame. My sister and I join in our duty to my Father and Mother and love to yourself, I hope my mother won't be angry for my not writing to her. I designed it but had not time. I beg a long letter from you as soon as possible; I assure you tis very desirable and will be thankfully received by Sir, your affectionate sister, sincere friend, and servant, Anne Steele.[23]

Submission to suffering

Anne was rarely able to enjoy her quiet life in Broughton with full health. As we have mentioned, recurring malaria and a string of other problems meant that she often endured acute pain. Anne came to believe that this was a means of bringing her closer to God: she was forced to rely on him in prayer. In the early years she had to fight to maintain trust in the sovereignty of God; in later years she came to a calm, resigned contentment. The Particular Baptists' convictions regarding God's control of all things thus had a very practical outworking in her life. Several of her best hymns, and those that have remained in use, take up the theme of providence (*extracts 11,12*). In 1762 she wrote to her sister-in-law who was also suffering severe illness:

> *Past experience affords great encouragement to look up with humble hope and trust to the kind Hand which hitherto hath helped us. I know that faintness and dejection of Spirit often attends long-protracted pain and weakness, but while the Eternal God is our Refuge, and underneath are the Everlasting Arms, we can never be utterly cast down. It was a good saying of Dr Watts in his sickness 'The Business of a Christian is to bear the will of God as well as to do it' but in this part of the Christian's duty as well as in all others we have need (in a conscious sense of our own weakness) to pray for a firm and constant assurance in Almighty power and goodness... Perhaps if our path were always smooth and easy and we met with no cold*

> *storms or distressing accidents we should be*
> *ready to sit down or at least loiter by the way,*
> *and be forgetful of our journey's end.*[24]

It is from the diaries of Mrs Steele, Anne's stepmother, that we get a glimpse of the terrible pain that Anne suffered for much of her life. Effective painkillers were unknown, and the 'means' the doctors used often exacerbated the suffering. Common remedies were bleeding (by knife or leech), purging, blistering (agonizingly painful, supposed to draw out bad bodily fluids), and inducing vomiting. All of this was a relic of the old belief that sickness was the effect of an imbalance of 'humours' or bodily fluids. It is truly pitiful to read of Mrs Steele's fervent prayers that such 'means' would procure relief. Her diaries give a fairly consistent picture of Anne's recurring fevers, pain, stomachache and toothache. Malaria sometimes brought on fits caused by extremely high fever, and eventually resulted in a nervous disorder.

For example, when Anne was thirty-two, she was ill continuously for four months. Just one of many such diary entries by her stepmother reads: 'Nanny was extremely bad in her stomach, her groans seemed to pierce me. I cry therefore to her God and my God that he would pity, ease and support her and sanctify the stroke.'

When Anne was thirty-four her health was so bad that she went to Bath with her sister for the months of May and June in order to 'take the waters'. The visit was not especially happy, as Anne was too ill much of the time to bathe or even to drink the waters. She was ill for much of her thirty-seventh year. When she was forty there are the first indications of a nervous disorder (which fits with the diagnosis of malaria), and at age forty-three the first indications of shortness of breath. From then on, until she was fifty-four, there were fluctuating periods of good and bad health, and from the age of fifty-four until her death six years later she was effectively housebound. Anne's own experience of suffering, and her conscious acceptance of it from the hand of God, meant that her poems and hymns on this theme struck a real chord with other sufferers.

Publication of her hymns — under the pseudonym 'Theodisia' (1760)

Anne's father was incredibly active: running a prosperous business, and yet also pastoring the Broughton chapel and helping with other local Baptist causes when they were without regular ministry. He encouraged Anne's writing. Her hymns were written in the first instance for her own devotional use, but then her father used many of them in the worship services at Broughton.

When Particular Baptist chapels began using hymns to supplement metrical psalms, they often used Isaac Watts (*Hymns and Songs*, 1707; *Psalms of David*, 1718).[25] His hymns were magnificent, but there were themes that he did not treat. Many ministers resorted to putting the theme of their sermon into rhyme (of varying quality). Anne was able to help her father by providing a steady stream of competent hymns well adapted to different occasions and themes, and her hymns were 'road-tested' at Broughton before being used more widely.

In 1760, when she was forty-three, a two-volume set of Anne's hymns and poems was published. As was common at the time, she used a pseudonym, and she chose the classical name 'Theodisia'. Nine years later the *Bristol Collection* was published, which included a number of

Anne's hymns. It became one of the most popular Baptist hymnbooks — widely used by Particular Baptists prior to the publication of *Rippon's Selection* in 1787. We may safely assume that the doctrine contained in Anne's hymns was acceptable to the wider body of Calvinistic Baptists, and it is interesting to note that she was uninhibited in writing of the free offer of the gospel (*extract 5*).

Anne's hymns never reach the perfection of some of the greatest hymns of Charles Wesley or Isaac Watts. But by the same token her hymns never plunge to the depths of some of the worst hymns of even the greatest hymn-writers.[26] Her hymns were of a steady, modest, fairly uniform character. They were above all usable — as a pastor's daughter she always had the needs of the congregation in mind. She provided hymns on the whole range of topics useful in public worship: baptism, the Lord's Supper, the three persons of the Trinity, the free offer of the gospel.

Some of Anne's hymns seem introspective and rather dour. In relation to her own state she often uses words such as gloomy, feeble, drooping, depressed, fainting, oppressed (*extract 12*). But this is only an honest portrayal of the feelings of one who is experiencing pain and sorrow. She responds by contemplating heavenly realities, and then uses the contrasting vocabulary: cheerful, rapture, radiant, joyful, exalted. The appeal of Anne's hymns and poems is the transparent honesty with which she confessed to struggling as a Christian. But she disciplined herself to react by looking forwards and upwards to heavenly realities.

To a modern ear, the metre of Anne's hymns can seem tedious. But the metre she used was simply the convention of the time. Congregational singing began in the sixteenth century with metrical Psalms. When hymns were introduced

We look not at the things which are seen ——
For the things which are not seen are Eternal.
                                    2 Cor. 4. 18.

*An engraving of the 'Muses' which illustrated volume II of the
original 1760 edition of Anne Steele's poems*

in the seventeenth century, hymnwriters began by para-
phrasing the psalms, then moved on to writing hymns
which fitted one of the three standard metres used for the
psalms: common, short or long.[27] Anne also put a good
number of psalms into verse, using these metres.

In 1780, two years after her death, her two-volume set
was reissued with an additional third volume of poems and
prose.[28] The introduction was by the well-known Baptist
Dr Caleb Evans, one of Anne's long-time friends and
correspondents. There were 105 hymns included in this
edition (as well as fifty-two psalms in verse). Her hymns
and poems were republished in 1863 with a memoir by
John Sheppard.[29] Anne became one of the best-known
Baptist hymnwriters of the eighteenth and nineteenth
centuries, and the Strict Baptists published a collection of
her hymns in the twentieth century.

The family circle broken (1760–1778)

The family circle was broken when Mrs Steele died in
1760. She had been a conscientious and devoted wife
and mother. Anne, aged forty-three, took over the running
of the home and the care of her ageing father. For the next
nine years, 1760 to 1769, until she was fifty-two, Anne
was not only writing her poems, hymns and essays, but
acting as housekeeper and nurse.

The next blow fell in 1762. Her brother William's wife
Mary died. Anne had been a constant visitor to their nearby
home. Mary had been a friend as well as a sister-in-law,
and, of course, Anne was devastated on William's behalf
as well as her own. William was left with a young daughter
to take care of. Like his father he was often away on
business, and the day-to-day care and education of nine-

year-old Polly fell to Anne. Although William later remarried, Polly remained devoted to her Aunt Anne, regarding her as a mother.

The bitterest loss came when Anne's father died in 1769, one month before his eightieth birthday. He had preached at Broughton for sixty years, and delivered his last sermon two weeks before his death, with 'his usual propriety and animation'.[30] Anne had poured out her affection on him, and his death left a great void in her life. She had lost both a father and a pastor. The house was packed up, and she moved in with her brother William and his second wife. (Nathanael Rowlings, who had studied at Bristol Baptist Academy, was called to pastor the chapel in 1772 and ministered there until 1777).

Just three years after her father's death, Anne's younger half-sister Mary died in 1772 at the early age of forty-eight. She left three children. Anne was close to these children, and felt their loss deeply as well as her own. 'Amira' had been not just a sister, but a spiritual sister and a good friend. Now only brother William was left. He continued to be a loyal friend. He and his second wife lovingly cared for Anne when a couple of years later her health finally broke down — she lived as an invalid for her final six years, until her death at the age of sixty. During the last year she suffered a measure of deafness, and William's letters mention 'lucid intervals' — indicating a measure of mental confusion — again, probably a result of her recurring malaria.

Anne died in 1778, just six years after her younger sister. She was mourned by her brother, his second wife, her nieces and nephews, the chapel circle and many friends. She was as yet unknown to the wider Christian public, since her poems and hymns had appeared under her pen name 'Theodisia'. This anonymity was just what she had wanted during her lifetime. Two years after her death, her identity became public knowledge when Caleb Evans republished her poems and hymns.

Her character and significance

Cheerfulness was the keynote of Anne's character. She aimed to give pleasure to those around her, even when she was suffering herself. Friendship and family solidarity were very important to her. In her earlier years she was over-sensitive: her letters reveal her fretting about her parents' health when she was away from home, worrying about whether she was pleasing them. But in later years she became more serene, less anxious about the opinion of others. Her family letters are warm, aiming to keep connections, aiming to keep the family united. She loved her nieces and nephews dearly. For example, an affectionate letter to Billy and Sammy (aged about seven and eight) in 1760 urges, 'Let not Billy tease or vex Sammy' or 'assume any insulting airs' (as an elder brother is prone to do), and urges Sammy to be patient with Billy and not feel bad because he is the younger.

Anne was genuinely humble. She knew that the material comforts she enjoyed were a gift from God: that her relatively comfortable status was nothing to be proud of. She knew too that her writing ability was also a gift from

God, and when complimented tried to point away from herself. She had a mind hungry for learning, and instilled a love of learning in her niece Polly.

Her humility enabled her to be patient through suffering. She did not grow resentful; she did not think that she 'deserved' a more comfortable life. Polly described how, in extreme sickness, she was still more concerned for others: 'In agony attentive ... anxious still for others' happiness.'[31]

Anne's genuine piety did not make her gloomy. She was ready to join in light-hearted fun, and her letters are witty and humorous. But she always remembered that life is short, and that we must be ready to face God. Writing to her little niece Polly one New Year, she characteristically exhorted her not only to think of the New Year, but also to prepare for eternity (*extract 13*). Polly should never begin a day without asking God for grace and help. Anne lived out this advice. She relied moment by moment on God for grace, and in her writing tried to encourage others to do the same. As she grew in intimacy with God, she became more independent of the opinions of others. Her greater confidence enabled her to take on responsibility for others in the family, in contrast to her dependence on others when she was younger. Anne demonstrated that even in suffering, a Christian can experience true happiness and contentment.

She also demonstrated contentment in singleness. What is more, her light-hearted and good-humoured discussions of marriage and singleness dispel any notions that eighteenth-century Nonconformists were dour or humourless.

Anne played a significant role in the development of eighteenth-century hymnody. First under her pseudonym 'Theodisia', and then after her death under her own name, she was probably the best-known Nonconformist female hymnwriter.

During Anne Steele's life, worship at Broughton Chapel seemed to go on untouched by the drama of the Wesleyan revival. But revival preachers stressed 'vital' or 'personal' religion, and chapels such as the one Anne belonged to taught this right through the eighteenth century. Testimony of personal conversion was a prerequisite for membership. Anne and her family spoke openly about their religious experiences, and regarded this as altogether normal. John Wesley's message seemed radically new to those in parish churches where morality was preached as the way of salvation, and where the clergy were plainly unregenerate. But personal assurance of forgiveness was a fundamental part of the message handed on by Dissenters such as the Steeles. We know that Anne's father and stepmother travelled to hear George Whitefield preach,[32] and the Baptist chapel did sometimes welcome itinerant Methodist preachers. So it was not isolated from revival influences. Certainly it would seem that by the end of Anne's life Broughton Chapel had become apathetic in evangelistic effort.[33] It was only in the period from about 1780 onwards (Anne died in 1778) that there was a tremendous flourishing of evangelistic efforts among Calvinistic Baptists and others, and the beginning of enthusiasm for overseas mission.[34] The reality of Anne's devotion gives a vignette of chapel life at a time during which steady perseverance rather than revival excitement was the norm.

Selections from her writings

Extract 1: Letter to her parents

This is part of a letter written to her stepmother from boarding school, when Anne was twelve:

...am sorry to hear of my Brothers illness, & Aunt's death. And doubt not but that my cousins are in a great deal of trouble for the death of their mother but I hope the same God that (no doubt) for wise ends took her from them will enable them to bear their affliction with patience. As to my liking the place, I suppose you know my mistress is an odd-tempered woman but she is as kind to me as to the rest, our work is most on headcloths, and I hope I shall learn very well. I think your acquaintances here are all well at present. I am thro' mercy in good health. Cousin Betty is sent for home which makes me a little dull to be without her.

*I long to see you all & hope I shall see my
Father in a little time ... this with my duty to
my Father and yourself and love to sister Molly
is from your dutyfull and obedient Daughter,
Anne Steele.*

p.s. *I desire you would excuse my bad writing being
by candle because we work till its darkness.*[35]

Extract 2: Letter to her stepmother

Anne (seventeen) and Molly (ten) have been staying with
their cousins. Anne writes to her stepmother to let her know
how they are getting on:

*Dear mother, ... you need not be in any trouble
for my sister for she enjoys her health very well
and tho' she wants to see her Father and mother
yet she is so perfectly well satisfied with being
at Haycomb that she begs you would give her
leave to stay all the winter which my Aunt
desired me to inform you of, that we might
know your pleasure before the time comes that
we are to go home. For my part tho' I like living here and love the company of my relations
extremely well yet I can't say but I long to be at
home to see my dear parents...*[36]

Extract 3: An evening at home

This lively poem gives a pen-portrait of a typical evening
at home, and shows that in pre-television days 'home-
made' entertainment was far from boring!

In a dirty cold village far off from the Joys
Of company Visiting Nonsense and Noise
Would you know how we shorten the dull
    wintry nights
And supply the sad want of those charming
    delights
A Candle is lighted and cheerful we sit
Close round a good Fire of odiferous Peat
Its fragrance inhaling delightful perfume
Which sweetens our Garments and fills all the
    Room
Our Needles employ us and chat miscellaneous
Or serious or trifling or News entertain us
And sometimes a neighbour may chance to
    come in
A Farmer or so to enliven the Scene ...
The Hours run along a full gallop or trot
And Supper postponed till 'tis almost forgot
But if uninterrupted sometimes we can find
Amusements much better than this for the Mind
When one of the company reads to the rest
Grave Author or Poet or what we like best
All soft and harmonious the hours glide along
Conversing with Pope or with Thompson or
    Young
When these I have named 'tis scarce needful
    to mention
That all sit delighted with eager attention
But to the sublime we can't always attend
I mean Polly and I for we sometimes descend
To capping of verses for Vanity's sake
And laugh at the whimsical Mixture we make.
Or if rhyming should happen our fancy to hit

Quick flows the extempore Nonsense or Wit ...
Thus reading and talking in work or in play
Imperceptibly slides the long evening away.[37]

Extract 4: Hymn of devotion

Anne's hymns were originally written for personal use. They were then used in the chapel at Broughton. Friends in her circle admired them, persuaded her to seek publication, and organized the details. James Fanch, a local Baptist minister, wrote, 'Her poetical compositions, both of the serious and amusing kind, are almost inimitable, much beyond anything I have seen since those of Dr Watts. She aims not at the sublime, or any high flights of imagination, but her productions are admirably correct and delicate.'[38] This is one of many hymns expressing devotion to Christ.

Come ye that love the Saviour's name,
And joy to make it known;
The Sovereign of your heart proclaim,
And bow before his throne.

Behold your King, your Saviour crowned
With glories all divine;
And tell the wondering nations round
How bright those glories shine.

Infinite power and boundless grace
In him unite their rays;
You that have e'er beheld his face,
Can you forbear his praise?

When in his earthly courts we view
The glories of our King,
We long to love as angels do,
And wish like them to sing.

And shall we long and wish in vain?
Lord, teach our songs to rise!
Thy love can animate the strain,
And bid it reach the skies.

O happy period! glorious day!
When heaven and earth shall raise
With all their power, the raptured lay
To celebrate thy praise.[39]

Extract 5: The free offer of the gospel

The Calvinism of the Particular Baptists did not preclude
firm belief in the free offer of the gospel. This offer is the
theme of 'The Saviour calls', still sung today. The final
verse expresses the equally firm belief in divine sovereignty,
and that sinners would not actually respond to the free
offer unless God enabled them.

The Saviour calls, let every ear
Attend the heavenly sound;
Ye doubting souls, dismiss your fear,
Hope smiles reviving round.

For every thirsty, longing heart,
Here streams of mercy flow;
And life and health and bliss impart,
To banish mortal woe.

Ye sinners come, 'tis mercy's voice;
The gracious call obey;
Mercy invites to heavenly joys,
And can you yet delay?

Dear Saviour draw reluctant hearts,
To thee let sinners fly,
And take the bliss thy love imparts,
And drink, and never die.[40]

Extract 6: The treasure of the Word

While those in the Established Church valued tradition as well as the Bible, Nonconformists were devoted to Scripture alone as their guide. This emphasis comes over strongly in several of Anne's hymns. 'Father of mercies, in thy Word, what endless glory shines!' still appears in some hymn-books, albeit shortened from the original twelve verses. The Bible is described as a mine of wealth, a tree of knowledge, a wonderful feast, a spring of life-giving water:

Father of mercies, in thy Word,
What endless glory shines!
For ever be thy name adored
For these celestial lines.

Here may the blind and hungry come,
And light and food receive;
Here shall the lowliest guest have room,
And taste and see and live.

Here springs of consolation rise
To cheer the fainting mind,

And thirsting souls receive supplies,
And sweet refreshment find.

Here the Redeemer's welcome voice
Spreads heavenly peace around;
And life and everlasting joys
Attend the blissful sound.

O may these heavenly pages be
My ever dear delight,
And still new beauties may I see,
And still increasing light.

Divine instructor, gracious Lord,
Be thou for ever near,
Teach me to love thy sacred Word,
And view my Saviour there.[41]

Extract 7: Marriage and singleness

Anne and her family and friends regularly exchanged correspondence in prose and verse using pen-names. Here, Anne (pen-name 'Silviana') mocks the 'happiness' of the married state, and her half-sister Mary (pen-name 'Amira') teases Anne ('Silviana') about the disadvantages of singleness.

Silviana
Ye happy kind Mortals ye Married folks say
When the other dear half of your hearts is away
If all the soft pleasures you talk of in love
Can balance the pains which in absence you
   prove

If you would but confess 'em how gloomy your
*   fears*
How great your anxieties troubles and cares
What endless perplexities torture your breast
Can happiness dwell in a heart without rest...
What scenes of distraction wild fancy supplies
And dangers and terrors from robbers arise...
Can passion and peace ever dwell in one heart
Fate has joined love and care and they never
*   can part.*

Amira [Mary]
Ye happy free mortals ye single folk say
Do you feel no pain don't your hearts run away
Sometimes from your reason and secretly love
Some swain whom your judgement can never
*   approve*
No doubt but in wedlock there's plenty of fears
But if they would own it han't single folks
*   cares...*
If our minds with strange whimseys wild fancies
*   supplies*
What terrors from wrinkles in yours must arise...
But as pride love and beauty are equally vain
And since Married or Single you'll surely find
*   pain*
As well you may peaceably yield up your heart
And in every care let a husband take part.

Silviana
If Spinsters with beauty must soon lose their sway
Wives give up their freedom in one fatal
*   day...*[42]

Extract 8: The 'meadow' of marriage

Anne has refused another proposal of marriage. Her step-sister has expressed her disapproval. It is high time that Anne, aged forty, conforms to social norms and gets married! Their letters on the subject are light-hearted, and use the analogy of a 'meadow' for marriage. Here, Anne continues the exchange:

> *No indeed my dear sister, I have no mind to climb the stile you point to [marriage], 'tis true a gentle swain with many soft entreaties lately offer' his hand to help me over, but I made him a curt'sie and declined his officious civility, for I looked over and saw no flowers, but observ'd a great many thorns, and I suppose there are more hid under the leaves, but as there is not verdure enough to cover half of 'em it must be near winter, as I think it generally happens when I look into the said Meadow...* [she goes on even more whimsically into verse].[43]

Mary responded:

> *Very well, and so my Dear sister's gentle Swain made a bow I suppose to your curtsie and drew back his gentle hand did he, alacka day how cou'd you be so uncivil? Why do we women folk often give our hand to be help'd over a stile tho' we cou'd do it better without, only for civility and custom sake, and why pray shou'dn't you conform to the custom as well as other folk? but you have no mind to get over because you*

*see thorns instead of flowers on t'other side,
why, don't flowers grow on thorns at all times
of the year? Tho' I fear it isn't so in my meadow,
it doubtless woul'd in yours, tho' I question
whether your feet might not stick in the dirt a
little and hinder your entertainment in those
fine groves, yet if this gentle Swain shol'd
notwithstanding your curtsie and his bow, again
softly entreat you to take his offer'd hand and
hold it out till it aches, shou'd you not take pity
on him and consider — and consider of it till
you consent in a very staid manner to trudge
along together on as pleasant a walk as the
nature of the road will possibly admit of. If not
I wish you well in your present path, and in your
frequent journey to those evergreen Groves.*[44]

To which Anne replies in forthright manner:

*Sure Amira [Mary] shou'd have consider'd a little,
before she charg'd so compliant a person as her
Sister with incivility. Suppose you are walking
thro' an extensive Field in a fine even path all
alone, enjoying the still evening in a
Contemplative humour, and you meet a Person
who has a mind to walk in a Meadow just by
(tho' I don't know whether a thorny Coppice
woul'd not be a better Simile) and he insists on
your leaving your path to go with him because
forsooth he likes your Company. You make him
a Curtsie — No Sir — I like my own path better
— I choose to be alone — doubtless you may
meet with others who wou'd be glad of your*

*company — I beg you wou'd not importune me
— adieu Sir — pray wou'd this be unmannerly?
— well, suppose he is loth to depart, and teases
you, and holds out his hand again till it aches
as you say — wou'd you not rather of the two,
that his hand ached than your heart? Charity
begins at home you know — and so my dear I
thank you for your good wishes but choose the
last of your IF's —but seriously the aforesaid
Swain is Good and worthy Man and I sincerely
wish him happy...*[45]

Extract 9: Content in her singleness

Here Anne teases 'Melinda' (possibly a pseudonym, maybe
for her half-sister) about her visit to town and the admirers
she collected. In contrast Anne refers to herself as a 'nun'
and her rural room at home as a 'cell' — a light-hearted
reference to her single state.

*To Melinda
From driving rattling up and down
Amid the pleasures of the Town
Elate with Conquest (fate how glorious)
Melinda now returns Victorious
Three hearts subdued too much by half
D'ye think such News can make me laugh
While I, poor solitary Nun
Moping at home can't rise to one
Three the News says and one before
'Tis some time since you counted four
You make such haste it must be more
Perhaps by this time half a score*

Methinks 'Twould be but just and due
To spare your Sister one or two
But this is only spoke in jest
On second thoughts and those are best
Your Vict'ry since I cannot share
I want no slaves that you can spare
Lone quiet in a humble Cell
Will suit my temper full as well...[46]

Extract 10: Created for glory

Here Anne expresses in verse her deep conviction that human beings were created for something far more noble than the trivia of everyday life.

The Fett'red Mind
Ah! Why should this immortal mind,
Enslav'ed by sense, be thus confin'd,
And never, never rise?
Why thus amus'd with empty toys,
And sooth'd with visionary joys
Forget her native skies?

The mind was form'd to mount sublime,
Beyond the narrow bounds of time,
To everlasting things;
But earthly vapours cloud her sight,
And hang with cold oppressive weight
Upon her drooping wings.

The world employs its various snares,
Of hopes and pleasures, pains and cares,
And chain'd to earth I lie:

> *When shall my fetter'd powers be free,*
> *And leave these seats of vanity,*
> *And upward learn to fly*...[47]

Extract 11: God's providence

Anne's own experience inevitably shows through: many of her hymns speak of trust in God's providence even through times of pain and weakness.

> *When I survey life's varied scene,*
> *Amid the darkest hours,*
> *Sweet rays of comfort shine between,*
> *And thorns are mixed with flowers.*

> *Lord teach me to adore thy hand,*
> *From whence my comforts flow;*
> *And let me in this desert land,*
> *A glimpse of Canaan know.*

> *And O, what'er of earthly bliss,*
> *Thy sovereign hand denies,*
> *Accepted at thy throne of grace,*
> *Let this petition rise:*

> *Give me a calm, a thankful heart,*
> *From every murmur free,*
> *The blessings of thy grace impart,*
> *And let me live to thee.*[48]

Extract 12: A calm resignation

The same theme of providence characterizes the hymn 'My God, my Father, blissful name'. This hymn expresses the calm resignation that characterized her later years.

My God, my Father, blissful name!
O may I call thee mine;
May I with sweet assurance claim
A portion so divine?

What'er thy providence denies
I calmly would resign,
For thou art just and good and wise;
O bend my will to thine!

What'er thy sacred will ordains,
O give me strength to bear;
And let me know my Father reigns,
And trust his tender care.

If pain and sickness rend this frame,
And life almost depart,
Is not thy mercy still the same,
To cheer this drooping heart?

If cares and sorrows me surround,
Their power why should I fear?
My inward peace they cannot wound,
If thou, my God, are near.[49]

Extract 13: Letter to Polly

Anne wrote as follows to her young niece one New Year:

My Dear Polly,
It is a common compliment at this season to
wish a happy New Year, but my wishes for you
reach further than a year, beyond the short rev-
olution of time, which will soon pass away. I
wish for you, my dear, a happy Eternity! The
only way to it is by the saving knowledge of
Jesus Christ, as you read in your Bible, 'Whom
to know is Life Eternal.' O that your mind may
be early improved by divine Grace with a sense
of your need of this almighty Saviour and that
you may be enabled to believe in him and obey
him ... don't go to bed one night or come down
one morning without praying to God for his
Grace. This advice I have given you before, but I
fear you do not think of it constantly, and wish
that this letter may help you to remember it.
I am, my dear Polly,
your truly affectionate aunt.[50]

FRANCES RIDLEY HAVERGAL

1836–1879

Lower Parade & Euston Place, Leamington Spa, circa 1843

Key dates & places

1836 Birth of Frances Ridley Havergal

1848 Mother died

1853 Confirmation

1861–1867 Governess for her sister's children

1867 Move to Leamington Spa

1869 *The Ministry of Song* published — the first of many books

1873 Experience of consecration

1878 Move to South Wales

1879 Death of Frances

Lichfield

Birmingham

Leamington Spa

Worcester

London

England

*F*rances Ridley Havergal was born just six months before Queen Victoria succeeded to the throne. Her life encapsulated many features of Victorian evangelicalism, and she became a spokeswoman for this movement through her phenomenally popular hymns, poems, devotional booklets, stories for children and daily devotional notes. Publishers vied with each other for her poems and articles. She died at the early age of forty-two. Her popularity increased after her death as her devoted sister Maria continued to edit her writings for publication. 'Take my life' is one of the most popular hymns of all time. Other favourites written by Havergal include: 'Lord speak to me, that I may speak', 'Master, speak, thy servant heareth', 'Like a river glorious', 'Who is on the Lord's side?' and 'I am trusting Thee, Lord Jesus.'

The setting

Victorian England was permeated with evangelical influence, and life, for evangelicals, was serious. Every moment of every day had to be accounted for — a theme captured in the hymn 'Take my life':

Take my life, and let it be
Consecrated, Lord, to thee,
Take my moments and my days,
Let them flow in ceaseless praise.

The life of its author encapsulated the religious seriousness of the age. Frances Ridley Havergal — along with tens of thousands of other earnest Christians — taught Sunday school, gave out food and clothes to the poor, collected for missions, distributed tracts, wrote countless letters on spiritual themes and visited the sick.

Frances was born in 1836, by which time, thanks to the Industrial Revolution, England was already becoming the 'workshop of the world' and was set on a course of great prosperity. This prosperity was not yet enjoyed by the multitudes of poor men, women and children who laboured in the mills and factories, or provided 'slave labour' in the workhouses. Whereas village populations were at least theoretically cared for spiritually by the parish priest, vast numbers of people in the rapidly growing towns and cities were totally outside the influence of the church. Victorian evangelicals were convinced of the need to 'loudly and insistently'[1] take the gospel to the masses of urban poor.

Frances Havergal's father and two brothers were ordained in the Anglican Church; she, her stepmother and sisters worked alongside him in poor relief and evangelism.[2] The parish was the arena in which every member of the family could do good. While in Worcester, eight-year-old Frances made friends with the daughter of the local MP and established the 'Flannel Petticoat Society'. The two little girls collected money from their friends, commissioned Frances' older sisters Maria and Ellen to pick out needy children, organized the sewing of specially fitted clothes, and on 5 November each year had a party at the rectory where the poor children came in for new clothes and cake. While this sounds patronizing to modern ears, we have to remember that in pre-welfare-state days the vicarage was often open at all hours as a lifeline to help desperately needy people. Society was rigidly stratified — all knew their place. When nine-year-old Frances took her first Sunday school class, her six-year-old pupils all dropped her a curtsey before sitting down.

If the Established Church in the eighteenth century had been characterized by worldliness and complacency, all that had been changed by the massively powerful influence of the evangelical revival. Evangelical Anglicans such as William Wilberforce stressed the natural sinfulness of humans, and the need for a supernatural conversion. This is exemplified in the explanation Frances gave for preparing a brief autobiography towards the end of her life. What, she asked, if she were too ill on her deathbed to give the convincing 'evidences' of conversion that Victorian evangelicals were so anxious to secure? Would her loving relatives then agonize about her eternal destiny? The possibility seems so ludicrous when we look at the evident radiance of her life — but no, there had to be proof positive of actual *conversion*. Of course, conversion was only the start: evangelicals preached 'vital' or living religion. They expected Christians to examine their lives, to continually seek holiness, and above all to 'be useful', not only in material philanthropic terms, but in eternal spiritual terms. The Havergals were typical of evangelical Anglicans, in that they were devoted to the order of worship as laid out in the *Book of Common Prayer*; they opposed Catholicism; they firmly believed that establishment gave Christianity a rightful place of influence in the nation. While on holiday in 1869 Frances heard that 'that horrid wicked bill' (for the disestablishment of the Irish Church) had gone through the House of Lords, and was greatly distressed[3] — the injustice of demanding tithes for the support of the Anglican Church from the seven-eighths of the population who were Catholic would not have crossed her mind.

During Queen Victoria's reign, the rapid expansion of the railway network opened up travel possibilities both in Britain and on the Continent. Thomas Cook began organizing excursions in 1841, and by the 1860s and 1870s large numbers of the middle classes were enjoying trips to France, Switzerland and Italy. Frances visited the Continent in 1869, 1871, 1873, 1874 and 1876. Each time she recorded her daily experiences in 'circular' letters to her family members, and after her death they were edited and published. They make for delightful reading. Frances loved meeting different people, and she was able to converse fluently in German and French. She had an eye for the humour in any situation, and her vivid descriptions are lively, funny, and show her love of beauty in many things, whether in the grandeur of mountains, the loveliness of tiny flowers, the expression on a child's face, or the cleanliness of Swiss chalets. Her letters found a ready audience. Just as an appreciative American public pounced on Harriet Beecher Stowe's *Sunny Memories of Foreign Lands* (1854), using Stowe's holiday diaries almost as a guidebook for the new pastime of visiting Europe, so Havergal's admirers were able to learn about the new possibilities of Continental travel from her *Swiss Letters*, and pick up tips as to where to go, what to do and even what to wear.

Woven through the *Swiss Letters* are numerous anecdotes of personal witness. Frances seemed to make friends effortlessly with fellow travellers, hotel maids, workers in the fields and mountain guides. She constantly shared the gospel and gave out tracts. Nothing typifies the zeal of Victorian evangelicals better than a piece Frances wrote after one continental holiday entitled 'Holiday Work'.[4] She directed her essay to over-tired Christian workers, urging them to escape to the beauty of the Alps as a tonic for mind, body and spirit. She explained how they could do the trip economically (eight weeks' travelling for well under £25). Some tender consciences might not be able to justify even a modest outlay but she assured any such that there were wonderful opportunities for evangelistic work and gave testimony of how she witnessed to many people on every day of her trip. For example, when she and her friend Elizabeth passed through a Paris torn apart by war they spent nearly three hours giving out tracts:

> *Such eagerness for the little books, such gratitude, such attentive listening as we tried to talk of Jesus, such tears as we touched the chord of suffering, still vibrating among these poor people, to whom war had been an awful reality! Surely God sent us! ... We went into a large room where several wounded soldiers lay ... here again all was earnest attention and gratitude... As we returned through the town we found many waylaying us. At one point ... at least thirty persons were waiting, and pressed around us begging for more tracts...*[5]

At every inn they stayed in they spoke to the maids, and gave out Gospels in their language with key texts marked up. While out walking they went to groups of hay-makers, spoke to them, and gave tracts. They memorized verses in French and German, to share with others. Frances graphically described the spiritual darkness of the Catholic cantons of Switzerland, and appealed for others to go and share the gospel with them. Thus, even a 'holiday' was regarded as an opportunity to 'do good' and 'be useful'.

A similar seriousness governed recreation. Frances loved reading, but limited herself to 'improving' books: theology, history, geography and some poetry. She shunned novels and plays, even Shakespeare. In a pre-TV era, entertainment was self-made: middle and upper class girls were trained to play and sing for the 'drawing room'. Frances limited herself to an almost exclusively 'sacred' repertoire, and used her musical ability as an evangelistic tool. 'Take my voice and let me sing, always, only for my King' was taken literally. Victorian evangelicals kept the 'Sabbath' rigorously. So when Frances was on holiday with her little niece Emily, and Emily noticed another little girl playing with dolls on Sunday, she persuaded the little girl to come and see her Aunt Frances to be put right. Frances focused on the gospel message — Christ and forgiveness. Emily later finished the work by explaining about the dolls!

Every period of renewal in church history seems to have been accompanied by the composition of fresh hymns and songs. The evangelistic crusades of D. L. Moody and Ira Sankey in 1873 and 1874, the various strands of the 'holiness' movement, and the start of the Keswick Convention in 1875 were only the most visible manifestations of the new spiritual enthusiasm that was experienced by Christians in various denominations and groups. Frances Ridley Havergal's hymns, especially those on the themes of consecration and holiness (*extracts 3,5,8,10,11,13*), arose out of this time of spiritual renewal, and gave expression to it.

The story

Childhood, education, confirmation, church work (1836–1860)

Frances spent her childhood in a beautiful area of the country: her father was rector in Astley, Worcestershire. The spacious rectory had acres of grounds and the family enjoyed outstanding views of the lovely Malvern Hills. She was the youngest of six children. Miriam, Maria, and Ellen were nineteen, fifteen and thirteen when she was born; her brothers Henry and Frank were sixteen and seven. As the baby of the family Frances was the delight of her father, whose nickname for her was 'Little Quicksilver', pointing to her bright but highly strung disposition. One curate noted, 'She was her dear mother in miniature especially in the brightness of her expression and the sparkle of her eye.'[6] She evidenced a sunny nature from the very earliest years; and inherited the family love for music. Her father William Havergal was a distinguished church musician, who composed many hymns and chants. Frances was also exceptionally bright. She could read at the age of three, and soon learned French and German. Her first little hymn was written at the age of seven. Her early academic feats are truly remarkable, and by the time she was twenty she had memorized great sections of Scripture, including many of the epistles, the Gospels, Isaiah, the Psalms and Revelation: some sections in the original Hebrew and Greek.

Frances described her early years in an autobiography, written shortly before her death. Evangelical parents wanted, above all else, evidence that their children were converted. Frances' mother wrote her a letter when she was away from home at the tender age of four. It included:

You remember the three little babies at Dunley. Jane, the one that you nursed is gone to heaven. May my Fanny know and love Jesus Christ! Then she will be sure to go to heaven whether she dies young or old.[7]

The trouble was that Frances knew that she was not converted. A sermon on hell, heard at a young age, haunted her day and night. She envied her older sisters with their confident assurance. She worried and fretted, and reacted by behaving naughtily out of sheer tension. She despaired, saying that conversion became less and less 'hoped for' and more and more 'longed for'. She noted in her autobiography that she never ever doubted her own sinfulness. But apart from this inner restlessness, the Astley years were very happy ones. She had free access to the surrounding beautiful countryside, and she developed a deep and enduring love of nature. The family moved from Astley when she was five, and for the next three years or so they lived at Henwick House, in Hallow, near Worcester.

In 1842 Frances' eldest sister Miriam was married and moved away: a terrible blow for the little girl then aged six. Miriam had been her teacher, but more than that, she more than any of the others had been her friend, and had taken a sensitive, non-patronizing interest in all her concerns. After Miriam left home Frances was intensely lonely:

> *Being a 'youngest' by so many years, and not knowing many children, I very rarely had a companion except my little Flora [her pet dog], in that large Henwick garden where I first learned to think; and that may be the reason why trees and grass were so much to me. They were the first pleasant leaf in God's great lesson book with me.*[8]

When Frances was nine, her father took up a position as rector of a large parish in Worcester, that of St Nicholas. He was also given the honorary position of canon. Frances was devastated when the family moved from the country to a gloomy house in the middle of town. Instead of fields and woods, there were narrow streets and crowded houses. Then another terrible blow: the death of her mother in 1848 when Frances was only eleven. She was unable in any way to see God in this awful sadness, and felt isolated in her grief.

At the age of thirteen Frances left home for a girls' school. The rigour of education at the time may be seen in that French was to be spoken at all times, and an average of eighty lines was to be memorized each day. Even though she was there only for one term, it was here that Frances really blossomed. Under the influence of a pious headmistress, who was making the most of her opportunities in the final term before her retirement, the atmosphere at Great Campden House, Kensington, was spiritually charged. Although Frances did not have a dramatic conversion experience, she began to feel something of the presence of God that she had longed for so badly. When the school closed, Frances had to leave. It was during a stay with her sister Miriam that she spent some time with an old family friend, Caroline Cooke. Caroline proved to be the one able to give Frances the encouragement and help she needed to make an open profession of faith. Soon after this, her fifty-eight-year-old father married the thirty-eight-year-old Caroline. This marriage would later cause some tension. Frances' beloved father was in effect marrying one of her friends. Perhaps Caroline sometimes felt left out by the closeness of the relationship between William and his favourite child, particularly when they collaborated on various musical projects. Her possessiveness towards her husband seems at times to have become obsessional: at all events Frances found her patience sorely tried.

In 1852 Frances went abroad with her father and stepmother, and she was able to spend some time boarding at a Prussian 'gymnasium'. She maintained a clear Christian testimony, although there seem to have been no other dedicated Christians, and the atmosphere was very different from what she had been used to in England. She excelled in her studies. Later, when she was staying with a German pastor in order to further her studies, he wrote:

She showed from the first, such application, such rare talent, such depth of comprehension, that I can only speak of her progress as extraordinary. She acquired such a knowledge of our most

celebrated authors in such a short time as even
German ladies attain after much longer study...
What imprinted the stamp of nobility upon her
whole being, and influenced all her opinions,
was her true piety, and the deep reverence she
had for her Lord and Saviour, whose example
penetrated her young life through and through.[9]

On returning to England, Frances was confirmed. She was then aged seventeen. This made a profound and lasting impression on her, and was an opportunity for renewed consecration. The following months and years saw her diligently continuing her studies, helping her stepmother and sisters in the benevolent work of the parish, and involved in Sunday school work. She took a detailed interest in her pupils, and some of the more earnest ones came to her during the week for individual Bible reading and prayer. She excelled in this kind of one-on-one personal work. Her Sunday school register served as a daily prayer diary for her scholars, and she noted in the last page of the register when her father left St Nicholas' Church:

It has been to my own soul a means of grace.
Often, when cold and lifeless in prayer, my
nightly intercession for them has unsealed the
frozen fountain, and the blessing sought for
them seemed to fall on myself. Often and often
have my own words to them been as a message
to myself of warning or peace ... seldom have
Bible truths seemed to reach and touch me
more than when seeking to arrange and simplify
them for my children.[10]

By the mid-nineteenth century the overseas mission movement was well underway — and it was dependent on enthusiastic 'home' supporters to raise funds and awareness. Frances was passionate about mission, and seems to have been unselfconscious in her fundraising efforts (*extract 6*). Indeed, one of the features of parochial visitation (in which she, her stepmother and sisters were constantly engaged) was the collection of mission funds from even the very poor. Not only did she raise funds herself for the Church Missionary Society and the Irish Society (a Protestant mission to Ireland), but she rallied youngsters to raise funds among their friends and families — organizing 'bands' of collectors who sent monies to her to be passed on, and encouraging them with circular letters, poems and stories. This ministry continued throughout her life.

Teaching, music, personal work (1860–1869)

When her father moved to the tiny parish of Shareshill in the diocese of Lichfield, Frances felt the break intensely, for she had become so involved in the parish work at Worcester. By this time she was twenty-three, and could not see a role for herself in this new parish, a tiny hamlet with a population of less than four hundred. Her father, stepmother, and her unmarried sister Maria could easily cope with the demands of such a small place. Frances went to live with her sister Miriam and her family at Oakhampton and stayed for the next six years, from 1861 to 1867. She acted as governess for two of the four children. And she enjoyed being back in the countryside: Oakhampton was in the Astley parish where she had spent her early childhood.

Frances sensed that perhaps she was called to a vocation in writing and music, and she longed to be a soul-winner. But her opportunities seemed limited to the mundane duties of the schoolroom and the routine of the family circle. She did do some writing, and three of her poems were published in 1860. During this time she was able to have professional singing lessons, and was in some demand as a soloist. She qualified as a singing teacher, and would find that this occupation in fact led to numerous openings for the evangelistic work she loved. Her years as a governess were also utilized in running 'evening classes for girls, visiting the cottagers, teaching in the Sunday school and personal evangelism in Astley parish and among her friends.'[11] She also continued to promote the work of the Church Missionary Society and the Irish Society. Any spare time was used for personal study: studying the Scriptures in the original Hebrew and Greek, and memorizing even more sections in English as well as some passages in the original languages.

Writing (1869–1879)

At the close of 1867, Frances' father retired, and decided to move to Leamington Spa. This town had sprung up in the early nineteenth century when 'taking the waters' became a popular health therapy, and after that fad passed it remained a genteel and attractive place, popular with retired army commanders, politicians and clergy. The Havergals moved into a comfortable Victorian home, 43 Binswood Avenue, which they named 'Pyrmont Villa'. Canon Havergal was able to preach in various local churches, and in the summer acted as chaplain at the continental resort of Pyrmont in the South of France.

It seems that Frances was no longer needed as a governess for her sister's children, and so she moved back in with her father and stepmother. From the start, she was active in the spiritual life of the town. She took singing classes (seen as an opportunity for personal evangelism), was involved with the YWCA, promoting mission and other good causes, and she led the choir at St Paul's. This was seen as far more than a musical task: she viewed music as a means of evangelism and encouragement, and she worked as much on the spiritual well-being of the choir as on their musical skill. Many wished to consult her about spiritual things, and she was frustrated by her stepmother's rule that she could not hold meetings or have visitors in her room: to have to submit to this when over thirty years old was very hard. Her father died the following year, and Frances, who had been devoted to him, was devastated. But her stepmother Caroline thought that Frances did not really feel the death of her father, because Frances kept her grief private, and was able to maintain an outward cheerfulness. Caroline's own grief seems to have changed her personality, and she began to exhibit symptoms of being seriously disturbed.

It was during the Leamington years that Frances saw her first book published. *The Ministry of Song* (1869) was to be the first of many published works: some poetry, some devotional (*extracts 15,16*), some for children (*extract 17*). She seems to have caught the mood of the time in style and content. Countless Christians found encouragement and inspiration through her writing. Seventeen publications appeared during the period from 1871 to her death in 1879, and then thirteen appeared after 1880. Many of them achieved wide circulation. There were also three musical works, and countless articles and poems in religious periodicals; equally numerous writings appeared in leaflet or tract form, or printed out on small gift cards. 'After her death, her popularity was so great that the market was flooded with small booklets containing selections from her prose and verse, often illustrated.'[12] Frances was also a prodigious letter writer.

She once said that 'I think God would teach me that a great deal of living must go to a very little writing,' and she regarded the trials of life as essential preparation enabling her to encourage others. Her writing was carried out in less than ideal circumstances. She was never allowed to feel that the house on Binswood Avenue was her own home. Caroline went away during summer months each year and when she did so the house was shut up and Frances likewise had to go away. When she was there during the winter, Caroline would only allow her to have a fire in her room once a week, so she generally had to do her writing downstairs, with all the interruptions that entailed. She longed for peace and quiet, but did not desire a confrontation with her stepmother on this issue.

Another source of tension at this time was the management of Canon Havergal's music and hymns. Mr Snepp, vicar of a parish in Lichfield, asked Frances' help in editing a work called *Songs of Grace and Glory*. He wanted permission to use two of Canon Havergal's published tune books. The problem was that 'Caroline Havergal's earlier possessiveness towards him [her late husband] assumed pathological proportions'[13] and she wished to re-edit all of his works herself, although she was not competent to do so. Somehow this problem was resolved. But when Frances had done all the work in editing Havergal's *Psalmody*, it was her stepmother who wanted to give her own name to it. This was hurtful.[14] By now Caroline was a constant trial and, Frances reckoned, somewhat mentally unbalanced. Despite all this Frances was able to work furiously on editing and composition, contributing some of her own hymns and tunes to the final *Songs of Grace and Glory.*

Her fluency in writing hymns during these years became legendary. She herself contrasted the ease of composition with her struggles in earlier years:

> *I have a curiously vivid sense not merely of my verse faculty in general being given me, but of every separate poem or hymn, nay every line, being given. (I never write the simplest thing now without prayer for help.) I suppose this arises from the fact that I cannot write exactly at will. I verily believe that I could not produce a poem to save my life, if I had to do it... It is peculiarly pleasant thus to take every thought, every verse as a direct gift... I had nothing of this impression when I wrote in 1859 and 1860.*[15]

Similarly she wrote:

> *Writing is praying for me, for I never seem to write even a verse by myself, and feel like a little child writing: you know a child would look up at every sentence and say, 'And what shall I say next?' That is just what I do; I ask that every line He would give me, not merely thoughts and power, but also every word, even the very rhymes. Very often I have a most distinct and happy consciousness of direct answers.*[16]

Some of her hymns are still well loved and much used. Perhaps the best-loved of all is 'Take my life,' to which Frances wrote a companion book, *Kept for the Master's Use (extracts 1,15)*. She used to take supplies of cards to meetings with the hymn printed out and a blank space for a signature. After explaining its meaning she would invite all who could sincerely sign to do so.

Frances' writing career was marked by several disappointments. After she had poured so much energy into the editing of her father's musical work, her stepmother would not allow Frances to put her name on the preface (which Frances had written herself). Rightly or wrongly, Frances saw this as potentially robbing her of an introduction into the field of Christian music. A far bigger blow came when the American publisher (whom she had given sole rights to her works in the USA) suffered sudden and total bankruptcy. Frances regarded this as the 'end of all her prospects' in America. Worst of all, in 1875 she sent a manuscript to her publishers — an appendix to her *Songs of Grace and Glory* with music for the hymns, including many of her own compositions, as well as her harmonizations for the tunes of others. Within a week of her sending in the manuscript the premises of the printer burned down and all her work was lost. Every previous manuscript submitted had been laboriously copied twice by hand, so that she could keep a copy. This time she had decided not to bother. She had not even kept a list of the tunes, and now needed to work out the harmonizations from scratch, and try to remember her own melodies.

Frances took this as a lesson. She had rushed the project, so as to be able to get on with another book. She believed that the Lord was giving her an opportunity to do the work all over again — this time more patiently.

Frances Ridley Havergal

'Holiday Work'

The difficulties at home partly explain Frances' perpetual
travelling during these years. She loved the hills of Wales
(for example the precipice walk near 'Dolgelly'[17]) and also
the Lake District, but once she discovered the beauty of
Switzerland she could not resist returning time after time.
She could not understand how friends could keep visiting
the 'hot and hideous south coast and the towns that man
made' (i.e. Brighton!), when the 'beauty that God made'
could be reached relatively cheaply.[18] Frances certainly
found that the majesty of the mountains drew out deeper
appreciation for the power and glory of the Creator, and
much of her poetry was inspired by the magnificence of the
scenery there. She also felt tremendous physical benefits
from walking and climbing in the pure air. A whole volume
of the letters she wrote home during these trips was published after her death, *Swiss Letters and Alpine Poems*.
This volume also included the little tract 'Holiday Work',
which urged Christian workers to take time to travel and
relax, but which showed that such holidays could be great
opportunities for witness. Frances was unhindered by
language barriers — she could speak easily, write hymns,
and deliver Bible talks in French and German — but she
gave plenty of tips about how to witness even without
the language.

Of all Frances' books, *Swiss Letters* is the one in which
her personality shines through. She wrote her letters for
family members, never thinking they would be published,
and she was uninhibited in her lively and humorous
descriptions. The letters were rapidly and beautifully written,
and very amusing (*extracts 21,22*). Frances found the
inevitable mishaps vastly entertaining, and phrases such

as 'we nearly died laughing,' 'we were in the very highest of spirits,' and so forth, abound. She revelled in throwing aside conventions. 'How we ... scrambled, and leaped, and laughed and raced.'[19] Or again, 'how horrified you would have been at my attire' she wrote mischievously to her eldest sister, 'on alighting we took off every single thing, even the skirts of our dresses, and I proceeded with simply my grey linen unlined bodice on, and not even a necktie, between four and five a.m., and over ice and snow.'[20] She loved swimming in a swimming bath joined onto the Rhone, where 'at one end the river comes in a regular waterfall three feet high, through which you can see the light, blue and shining ... it was such fun to swim down the long bath, it was one's beau ideal of bathing, and the cool, transparent, exquisite blue is so much nicer than salt grey waves.'[21]

Frances loved a challenge — long hikes, difficult climbs, and dangerous routes. She enjoyed the physical challenge of 'glissading', never minded getting soaking wet, and found it uproariously funny when she and her companions tried it when roped together — and ended up collapsing in a heap. She especially loved the times when they turned out at three or so in the morning to climb to catch the sunrise from some particular beauty spot. Climbing (in skirts!) was done with a guide, but walking could be done alone. A highlight of her 1874 trip was when she left her niece behind and took off for a three-day hike on her own. Knowing her stepmother would be horrified, she apologizes:

Please, nobody is to be shocked by this, because I quite came to the conclusion that it was not incorrect at all, and I found other ladies doing it. Besides, who is to be any the wiser? If one is

seen marching alone, one may have friends five
minutes before or behind for aught anyone
knows![22]

The various inevitable mishaps were regarded as highly entertaining. After one long hike she and Mr Snepp asked their host at an *auberge* (inn) whether a horse and carriage or any other conveyance could be hired to take them back to their hotel. To their amusement he went away and hastily assembled a makeshift rickshaw, which he pulled himself, on which they had a hair-raising descent ('our cheeks shook like jelly') and which fell entirely to pieces at the bottom of the hill. 'We extricated ourselves with nothing more than a bruise or two, laughing more than ever.'[23] During one train journey she left the train at one stop, only to get back to her carriage and find all her luggage gone. A time-consuming search of the entire station and all the empty carriages followed, in pitch darkness apart from a red lamp held up by a railway official. Far from panicking, she enjoyed the adventure: 'I could not help laughing at the position, dodging full tear in and out of sheds and across turning tables behind the red lamp, as if it were a will o' the wisp.'[24] Eventually the vanished luggage was found.

Frances enjoyed people wherever she went, and pre-ferred simple guest-house accommodation to the large hotels. The huge contrasts in catering between the two kinds of establishment was a source of amusement, and she sent her family detailed accounts of menus and prices. The regular *table d'hôte* menus in big hotels consisted of interminable courses, and she generally found them tedious, unless they were accompanied by music, as in the following:

Our table d'hôte was accompanied by a very
charming string quartet. I subjoin the 'Menu
Musicale':
Soupe Royale: to potpourri from Donizetti
Salmon trout with Dutch sauce and potatoes:
to a lively and pretty waltz
Roast beef and lettuce: to a fine solid thing of
Mendelssohn's
Calf's head en tortue: to a set of rubbishy
quadrilles
Mutton and green peas mashed: to — silence
Spinach and eggs à la créme: to Gounod's
Berceuse
Chicken and salad: to a plaintive and sweet
violin air
Lemon pudding: to Soldier's March in Faust
Gâteau Pithiviers and compote de pommes: to
a waltz by Strauss
Dessert: to another waltz by Strauss[25]

Perhaps it is not so surprising that she liked the informality
of picnic breakfasts (usually red wine, cheese and bread) at
the mountain lodges, or the simplicity of catering at the
auberges. In one such she was ushered through a 'little
dark kitchen with a pot hanging over a gypsy-like fire of
sticks on a great hearthstone' then through to a little 'salon'
with three little tables and six little benches. The host:

... scampered about getting the necessaries
together with the help of his equally good tem-
pered but quieter help-meet. First he produced
a bottle of Swiss wine, then a loaf of capital
black bread, and a plate with three funny little

cheeses and one knife... He offered an egg, and while it was boiling sent around the village for butter... Presently my egg appeared in a little brandy glass, but a spoon had not occurred to him... In the course of time the butter arrived, quite superlative and newly churned, so we were in clover.[26]

Frances was not fussy, but even she sometimes found the village food unpalatable:

At the little inn they brought us first a tureen of bright yellow soup, tasting like bad sour milk and oil, which even I could not touch! They call the compound 'egg soup'... Then they produced a tureen of dish water with a mild flavouring of broth, in which floated irregular slices and lumps of stale bread, with a few blacks and a good deal of smoke to improve the mess. So for once I really appreciated the table d'hôte on our return which is generally an unmitigated bore.[27]

Contrasts in cuisine were matched by contrasts in accommodation. On her 1873 trip with the Snepps, they stayed in the Grand Hôtel in Paris, supposedly the finest in Europe at the time:

... we go up and down in a lift, and we have rooms with balconies looking down into a fine boulevard, and so high up that we see over most of the roofs, and get less noise and dust. The inner court of the hotel is almost like an immense conservatory, tree rhododendrons in full flower

and other things; the saloons are gorgeous, with enormous crystal chandeliers and mirror panels, so arranged as to make the place look interminable, quite a fairy-land by gaslight.[28]

She found it much more fun to rough it, as during the dramatic 'first ascent of the season' at Chamouni, where they stayed in a little wooden mountain lodge en route, with no fire, so 'we warmed our feet in the oven'.[29]

Of course the main attraction for Frances was the scenery. She loved the Alps. After one trip she was hooked. A short extract from one of her very first letters on her first trip conveys her excitement:

So now the dream of my life is realised, and I have seen snow mountains. I always thought of eternal snow and perfect peace together, and longed to see the one and drink in the other. And I am not disappointed ... I never saw anything material and earthly which so suggested the ethereal and heavenly, which so seemed to lead up to the unseen, to be the very steps of the Throne.[30]

Her final trip to Switzerland was in 1876 with her sister Maria. Despite Maria's having to nurse Frances through a serious bout of illness, both were as zealous as ever to take opportunities to do good. Maria (who served full-time as a 'lady visitor' at home) described one incident illustrative of many others as follows: Out walking in the Val de Feri, they stopped for a picnic and Maria asked if there were any sick people in that place. A girl called Constance took her to a home where a little invalid girl was left alone all day while her father was out at work:

I followed Constance up some dark stairs into a room like a hayloft. A little tired face looked up from the rough bed... Alone, in that cold loft, some greasy soup in a can, and a hard crust! Dear little Aline. I sat down by her and fed her with some jelly and biscuits, and sent Constance for some new milk. I took the thin hot hand and said in French, 'Dear Aline, there is One who loves you very much, the dear, kind, Jesus. Do you know Him?' Yes, she knew the name of Jesus, and that he died on the cross, but she did not seem to know it really was for her, in her stead. She seemed to drink in all that was said, and learnt this prayer: 'Lord Jesus, wash me in thy blood, take me in thine arms.' I don't think Aline will be hungry again, for it was easy to arrange for a supply of milk. And Victorine, the daughter of our inn-keeper at Orsière, promised to go often and take her nourishing food. Meanwhile Frances had been at work in a chalet; I cannot recount half she does![31]

Frances also took the initiative to organize and speak at an impromptu evangelistic service in the village of Eizenflou:

Frances went to the school-master and secured the use of his school room for a service the next evening, as her spirit was stirred up by finding no pastor ever came near these villages, and they were five miles from church. The evening was wet, and I wanted Frances not to go; but she said, 'I may never come here again; and no man cares for these scattered sheep. The room was

quite full. Frances addressed them in German
from 1 John 1:7 and also led the hymns from
their chorale book. Our hostess' report was
'Never, no never, had anyone told them what
the dear young lady did; it was wonderful! They
never could forget her words; and surely she
must be a born German!'[32]

So holidays were regarded as opportunities to take the gospel to otherwise unreached places. After Frances' death, Maria added a concluding testimony to *Swiss Letters*. Maria revisited the Pension Wengen in 1878. The guide who had taken Frances up the Mettlen Alp and the Lauberhorn had died in a tragic accident earlier that year. During his final days, in agony, he witnessed to the doctors, and also to the rationalistic pastor who was brought in to attend him. He often spoke of Frances, and sang the hymn they had sung together at the top of the Lauberhorn. As a result, the pastor was converted, and began preaching evangelistically for the first time. The message was clear. 'Holiday work' would continue to do good, even after death.

'Consecrated, Lord to Thee' (1873)

The theme of Frances' life was consecration. Her favourite term for the Lord was 'Master' (*extracts 5,10,13*) and her joy was willing submission and obedience. This partly explains her contentment with her singleness. She received a number of proposals of marriage, but turned them down. She would not even have considered marrying a non-Christian, but probably would not have married someone who was half-hearted. This was not easy. She once wrote of the sense of 'general heart-loneliness and need of a one and special love ... and the belief that my life is to be a lonely one in that respect... I do so long for the love of Jesus to be poured in, as a real and satisfying compensation.'[33] As time went on she was able to write to a friend:

> *Ask the Lord if it is not his will you should marry to make you perfectly content, and then to take away all the wish out of your heart, so that you may be 'free to serve' with your whole mind undistracted by it. And then ask Him, in His great kindness that He would interpose in some way to make this easy to you, He has such wonderful ways!*[34]

Between about 1870 and 1876 various influences converged to produce a spiritual awakening in Britain. These years saw the continuation of the Mildmay Conference in London, D. L. Moody and Ira Sankey's visits from America in 1873 and 1874 (14,000 people filled the London Agricultural Hall to hear them) and the beginning of the Keswick Convention in 1875. Many Christians in various denominations and groupings were affected. T. H. Darlow comments: 'Souls that hunger and thirst after righteousness cannot remain irresponsive to the spiritual temperature and tension amid which their fellow-Christians are living and moving.'[35] And so it is no coincidence that it was on Advent Sunday 1873, just six years before her death, that Frances had an experience that was to affect her profoundly. It was a powerful awareness, such as she had never had before, of the cleansing blood of Jesus, and that having cleansed her Christ had the power to keep her, 'so I just utterly yielded myself to Him, and utterly trusted Him to keep me.'[36]

By nature Frances was a perfectionist, and constantly disappointed with her own spiritual performance. But on this day the text 1 John 1:7 seemed to speak to her in a new way. She suddenly grasped the significance of the present tense — the blood of Jesus cleanses us from all sin. As she wrote to her sister Maria:

> *It was that one word 'cleanseth' which opened the door of a very glory of hope and joy to me. I had never seen the force of the tense before, a continual present, always a present tense, not a present which the next moment becomes a past. It goes on cleansing, and I have no words to tell how my heart rejoices in it. Not a coming to be cleansed in the fountain only, but a remaining in the fountain, so that it may and can go on cleansing.*[37]

Some Christians claim to move onto a plane of 'sinless perfection', but it was just *because* Frances was so aware of her ongoing sin that she revelled in the certainty of on-going forgiveness. While some misread her experience, and suggested that she had joined those who claimed sinless perfection, she fiercely denied it. Rather, this renewed experience of consecration was the culmination of her prayer, 'Take my will ... my heart ... myself'. She wrote on Easter Sunday the next year:

> *Oh, it was so sweet, so glorious to see something of that, the being His own, the serving Him and pleasing Him, the being utterly at His*

disposal, and with Him, and in Him, and all for Him, on and on through ages and ages of eternity. My whole heart said, 'Whom have I in heaven but Thee? and there is none upon earth that I desire beside Thee!' [Psalm 73:25] It has been such a special day, that I cannot help hoping it may have been given, not for myself only, but to prepare me for some special message bearing, perhaps only one-to-one, perhaps to many while I am away. But I never feel eager even for that now; it is so much happier to leave it all with him, and I always pray, 'Use me Lord, or do not use me, just as Thou wilt.' Oh, he is so good to me, I really did not know six months ago that such unvarying peace was possible here... Only I wish everybody had it, and I wish good people would not think it their duty to stay in Romans vii, as I always conscientiously believed till of late! I cannot imagine how they can think that Rom. vii 25 and Rom. viii 2 could both describe St Paul's experience at the same moment. They seem so clearly consecutive and not contemporaneous. So 'Thanks be to God which giveth us the victory, through our Lord Jesus Christ!'[38]

Again, she wrote in May 1874:

The wonderful and glorious blessing which so many Christians are testifying to having found, was suddenly, marvellously sent to me last winter; and life is now what I never imagined life on earth could be, though I knew much of peace and joy in believing... It seems as if a call were going forth to His own children to make a more complete surrender of their whole selves and lives, and to enter into a fullness of consecration, which I for one had not realised before.[39]

And in October 1874:

So you too are being stirred up by the 'loving Spirit' to seek holiness and rest beyond that you have as yet found! Thank God! And I know not how to thank him enough that though only a year ago I knew absolutely nothing of this blessed life — had not read one word about it, — I can now tell you joyously that His own hand has led me into it, and that for nearly a year I have not known what it is to have a shadow of care in things temporal or spiritual, all is cast on Him and He gives me the victory and gladness in response to the utter trust (which is no less His gift); so that it is living a new life, and one which I really did not even suppose to be possible on earth.[40]

This was not merely an emotional experience but was rooted in the objective truth of the doctrine of union with Christ. She was now less dependent on her emotional ups and downs. Janet Grierson suggests that her spiritual life to this point had been characterized by striving 'for Christ'. She had been using all her gifts *for* him — speaking, writing, singing, loving — '[now] she found herself not only just *for* Christ, but *in* Christ, which meant that with St Paul she could now say "I can do all things through Christ which strengtheneth me."'[41]

This powerful sense of union with Christ seemed to liberate Frances. Certainly she felt more at peace with herself after this; it was as if a new life had begun. It was in the following year that she wrote her most famous hymn, 'Take my life' (*extract 1*). She herself explained the circumstances in which it was written:

> *I went for a little visit of five days* [to friends at Areley House, outside Stouport]. *There were ten persons in the house, some unconverted and long prayed for, some converted but not rejoicing Christians. He gave me the prayer, 'Lord, give me all in this house!' And He just did! Before I left the house everyone had got a blessing. The last night of my visit I was too happy to sleep, and passed most of the night in praise and renewal of my own consecration, and these little couplets formed themselves and chimed in my heart one after another until they finished with Ever, only, ALL for Thee!* [42]

The last years (1878–1879)

Frances nursed her stepmother through a critical illness, and Caroline died in May 1878. The house in Binswood Avenue was packed up and Frances took the opportunity of literally giving her silver and her gold to the Church Missionary Society. She moved to South Wales, to live with Maria and directed her energies towards temperance work, as well as writing and mission work. She was due to leave for a tour of mission stations in Ireland, when she became seriously ill in June 1879. Frances died at the relatively early age of forty-two. Since an attack of typhoid, caught on the Continent in 1874, she had been subject to feverish attacks. She sometimes had to take extended rest, but this was probably linked to her highly strung, hyper-sensitive disposition. She was mentally so active that when there was any strength to use she used it at full speed, and then was left shattered. But this final illness proved to be peritonitis, and the suffering was worse than anything she had experienced yet. Her sisters Maria and Ellen, and her brother Frank, were with her at the end. She asked that her favourite text be inscribed on her tomb: 'The blood of Christ, His Son, cleanseth us from all sin.' 'She whispered the names one by one of relatives and friends, adding the words, "I love them all... I want *all* to come to me in Heaven ... tell them 'Trust Jesus.'"' Ten minutes before she died, to the amazement of her gathered relatives, she summoned strength to sing the first verse of the hymn 'Jesus I will trust thee' to the tune she had composed. This simple verse sums up the beliefs on which she had based her whole life.

> *Jesus, I will trust Thee,*
> *Trust Thee with my soul,*
> *Guilty, lost and helpless,*
> *Thou canst make me whole.*
> *There is none in Heaven*
> *Or on earth like Thee,*
> *Thou hast died for sinners,*
> *Therefore, Lord, for me.*[43]

Her character and significance

Frances loved life, enjoyed people, revelled in nature and laughed a lot. Her enjoyment of life seems to have been somewhat hampered by Victorian propriety for much of the time, but she loved the relative freedom of holidays; for example on the Welsh coast where she could enjoy sea bathing, riding and climbing. Later in Switzerland she took delight in breaking convention and stripping down to her petticoat for a climb in the Alps. Her sense of humour sparkles all through the *Swiss Letters*. All kinds of events in her life, happy or sad, called out poems, and she was able to laugh at herself even in painful circumstances.

Those who knew her spoke of her warmth, charm, cheerfulness, affection and genuinely outgoing personality. There was a radiance and glow about her that could not be captured in any picture. Her brother-in-law commented that wherever she went, numerous individuals wanted to make appointments to see her. When she visited a large household, many members of the household — family, friends and servants — would seek her out to speak 'one-to-one' about spiritual things.

Certainly she was a child of her time, and limited in her perspective. She lived all her life in sheltered and pleasant environments: country parishes, the quiet cathedral town of Worcester, and the genteel spa town of Leamington. But her Continental travels did expose her to grimmer realities: during her 1871 European trip she met and spoke to victims of the 1870 Franco-Prussian war whose families had starved and who had lost homes and livelihoods (Paris was under siege from 19 September 1870 to 28 January 1871).

Yes, she shunned worldly activities such as balls, the theatre, opera or novels. But she loved music, and was a superb and sought-after performer. Her *Swiss Letters* give a marvellous running commentary on the sights and sounds of Continental Europe. She was evidently a lively, witty and sought-after person. She was single by choice, turning down several proposals of marriage.

Although she was always ready to give benevolent help on an individual level, there is little evidence that Frances had strong feelings about the blatant social and economic inequities of that time. The only wider political issues she ever took up with passion were the (religious) controversy over schools in the 1870s and, at the end of her life, the temperance movement. (While in earlier life Frances, along with most evangelicals of her time, was totally relaxed about drinking alcohol, by the end of her life she had become convinced of the social and moral evils of alcohol abuse). Other women of the time did campaign on social issues such as prostitution or slavery; not Frances.[44]

And yet the 'limiting' of her vision to gospel issues meant that she was extraordinarily focused (*extract 4*). Her mental and spiritual energies were not diffused into many different areas; her writing centred on the great issues of salvation, consecration and worship (*extract 9*). Her personal work always aimed to encourage others to move on in their knowledge of Christ (*extract 18*).

Frances was a perfectionist. She was hard on herself; many of her ups and downs seem to have been triggered by a sense of failure to meet the very high standards she set herself. Her Advent Sunday experience of the love of God seems to have helped to liberate her from this perfectionism. She subsequently enjoyed a real sense of being 'in Christ', which released her from striving in her own strength to please him. Normally perfectionists are also demanding to live with. Perhaps the tensions with her stepmother were exacerbated by her own intense personality and the high standards she set for herself and others. It is hard to tell, as Maria's editing of her letters and other sources is silent on anything negative.

Frances was an Anglican through and through, and seems to have mixed fairly exclusively in Anglican circles. She liked the Prayer Book service to be conducted in an orderly fashion, and became irritated if the chants were 'galloped through'. She particularly enjoyed choral cathedral services (if they were well done — any sloppiness in the playing or singing 'fidgeted' her). But she did visit Spurgeon's Tabernacle during one visit to London, and commented of the great Baptist preacher: 'I heard Spurgeon preach on Sunday AM, Magnificent! I don't recollect hearing anything finer.'[45]

The limitations of dependence

As an unmarried woman in Victorian society, Frances was 'dependent' on her father until his death, and then regarded it as her duty to submit to her stepmother until the latter's death. Only then (a year before her own death) did she feel free to make 'independent' decisions. Middle-class women were not expected to go out to work or have their own career. The only 'respectable' occupation open to them was that of governess. For six years Frances was governess for two of her sister Miriam's children, but while she loved children this was not the ideal use of her tremendous academic, musical and pastoral gifts. Before this, Frances had found scope for her pastoral and evangelistic gifts, but this was in her father's parish, so when he moved on her ministry ended. She spent much of her life as a visitor in the homes of her married brothers and sisters, and always threw herself into whatever benevolent or evangelistic work was available, but never had the stability of a home of her own or a recognized long-term ministry of her own.

While some middle-class women might be tempted to fritter time away, Frances disciplined herself to use 'all her moments and days' profitably. She had the drive and determination to learn French, German, Italian, Greek and Hebrew. Much of her education was acquired entirely on her own. She taught herself the discipline of harmony (a musical expert she visited on the Continent could hardly believe that she had not received formal instruction).

But Frances was not able to pursue music as a profession, and she was not able to settle to full-time Christian ministry either. Her real calling was writing, especially during her thirties, when she was based in Leamington (1867–1878). The publication of her first book in 1869 and the publication of her edited edition of her father's work gave her the confidence she needed to pursue writing. Yet the frustration of the Leamington years was that although she began making money from her writing, and offered to pay her own expenses, she was not allowed the freedom to do so by her stepmother.

The appalling and petty restrictions placed upon her at home explain Frances' continual travels during these years. She was among the first generation of British tourists to the Alps, and enjoyed five extended trips to Switzerland (in turn with her sister Jane, brother-in-law and niece; her best friend Elizabeth Clay; her friends Mr and Mrs Snepp and their daughter; a niece; and her sister Maria). She also travelled to Wales, the Lake District, to Ireland, and of course to her various married siblings.

To make things worse, Frances' strong sense of duty, tender conscience, and perfectionism meant that when she chaffed against her stepmother's restrictions she felt guilty. She wanted to love 'dear mother' and be the ideal dutiful daughter. Maria strongly urged her to leave Leamington and come and live with her. In reply Frances wrote:

I have had quite a struggle with my 'will' — I should so like the way to be opened up to come and live with you dear Marie. It is a very awkward position here — no freedom, always afraid to pay a call, or write a note without specifying. But I would never pain dear mother, or do anything she did not positively like. It seems most clear that I am placed here, and that without some most direct interposition of Providence, I should be doing wrong to leave, and could not expect a blessing... I never make the faintest opposition, or even counter-proposal, now to anything that dear mother arranges for me. I have long since determined, God helping me, there shall be no colour of excuse for saying that I am inconsistent ... it is quite right that I should learn to be invariably submissive to her.

*Outwardly I know I am absolutely so, but out-
wardly is not enough...*[46]

Was the biblical injunction to parental obedience being
taken much too far? Perhaps, yet she was being true to her
conscience, and the genuine spiritual struggles which all of
this evoked led to a deepening of her submission to God and
to great sensitivity to those in difficult family situations.
Perhaps if she had been in a more ideal situation (a place of
her own and independence to pursue a writing career or
another ministry) her writing would never have achieved such
depth and sensitivity. Her finest hymns and poems were
wrung out of painful trials (*extract 12*). Her life shows that
usefulness does not depend on being in ideal circumstances.

Personal work and 'living for the moment'

Frances set herself to 'live for the moment': to serve others
cheerfully in little ways and regard the trivial duties of each
day as sent from God. This gave significance to what would
otherwise have been a disjointed existence. Frances seized
every opportunity for 'personal work' — sharing the gospel
message with non-Christians (*extract 19*) and encouraging
Christians to trust Christ more fully. A large portion of her
writings treat this theme, and her letters give many examples
of her willingness to engage others — friends, contacts or
strangers — in spiritual conversation. She filled her 'spare'
time with correspondence, wanting friends and relatives
to 'go on' with the Lord (*extract 18*).

Frances used her musical ability in this cause too. She got
involved in several city missions: singing, giving testimony
(*extract 20*) and speaking about the meaning of the songs
she sang. At society parties, where it was customary for

ladies to play and sing, she would invariably sing a Christian
song, even if an embarrassed silence fell afterwards.

The term 'bridge-building' is often used to describe finding
common ground with people before sharing the gospel.
Frances used her music to build bridges, explaining to
a friend:

> *I think you judged me a little severely last autumn;*
> *you would not quite believe what indeed was*
> *the truth, when I told you that my music with*
> *_____ was not an end but a means. Indeed, my*
> *feeling in that duet-playing was very little for*
> *the music. I cared far less for that than you*
> *thought; I only thought it my fairest and likeliest*
> *means for getting intimate with _____, and*
> *gaining an influence over her. When she became*
> *willing to listen about better things, we gradually*
> *exchanged the practising for walks, so as to talk.*
> *Music was my grappling-iron only; it is not the*
> *first time it has been so, and as such I do desire*
> *to use it, and feel that if I neglected it entirely, it*
> *would be hiding a talent under a napkin.* [47]

But she was also prepared on occasion to be very direct:

> *The first opportunity I had, I only approached*
> *the subject sideways with _____. He probably*
> *saw what I was at, for he sheered me off so very*
> *quickly and pointedly to another topic, that I*
> *thought it best not to renew the attack, but*
> *adopt different tactics next time. So then I made*
> *a full front attack, which gave no chance of*
> *evasion, telling him straight out my fears and*

hopes and prayers for him personally. He staid [stayed] nearly an hour! arguing, cavilling and twisting about like an eel. He manoeuvred ingeniously to get me off Bible-ground, and entangle me in metaphysical thickets, but I know one is never safe but in standing firm on the Word and declining to use Saul's weapons — so he always found himself confronted with a smooth stone out the brook and thereby brought back again and again to personalities — 'And what about his own soul and salvation?' But I saw no impression; so far I have only delivered my own soul [an allusion to Ezekiel 2:19]. I think I was, however, enabled to speak winningly to him, and that he was a little touched by the reality of my anxiety for his salvation. He will be a real trophy for Jesus if converted... I was so exhausted after it, that I had only three quarters of an hour's sleep the whole night, having got quite overwrought.[48]

We have noted her continual evangelistic efforts whilst on holiday. For example, at Sunday dinner in a hotel in Heidelberg a good-looking young Italian (named Romeo) gave her his card. In turn she gave him one of her tracts:

...the table d'hôte was as un-Sunday an affair as possible, with a band playing most of the time in a very good style, beginning with the overture to 'Tancredi'! A little girl came around with flowers, a young gentleman sitting next [to] M.L. [Miriam Louisa, her niece], took a tiny bouquet of roses and pinks and laid it by her plate. He

did not speak English, and we had quite a talk in German. He was of Italian parentage (though of German abode), and had all the proper accompaniments of dark, handsome eyes, musical voice, and courteous manners. He wanted to arrange some excursion for us in the evening, but yielded politely at once when we declined [it was the Sabbath!]. Presently he offered me his card, 'Romeo Ghezzi'; I had not mine at hand, but what did much better, my Leaflets. So I chose out 'To whom, O Saviour shall we go!' and gave it to him, saying that was my card, having ascertained that he could read, though not speak, English. He read it slowly all the way through, asking me the German of two or three words he did not know, and then put it in his pocket book. He seemed a little taken aback at the style of the thing I fancy, but was too polite to make himself less agreeable for it, and for the few words with which it was followed up.[49]

Frances was very distressed if any of her acquaintances were influenced by the higher critical theories that were beginning to gain ground at this time:

And so in my quiet walks with dear _____ at Lynton and Ilfracombe, and with only our Bibles, I was enabled to guide her out of a very labyrinth of error (from reading Colenso and Essays and Reviews), and the subsequent gloom and unhinging of her faith and peace — truly it was Christ's recall to safe anchorage.[50]

She wrote a number of tracts, for Christians and non-Christians, which she gave out whenever possible. When staying in France, she wrote a hymn in French for an impromptu evangelistic service held by herself and sister Maria, and the indomitable Maria then took a copy of the hymn to the local priest as a pretext to engage him in conversation about the gospel.

The Romantic Movement

The nineteenth century was the century of the Romantic Movement — originating in Germany and carried forward in England by the poets William Wordsworth and Samuel Taylor Coleridge, and by the novelist Sir Walter Scott. It represented a reaction against over-reliance on intellect and reason (as in the so-called 'Enlightenment') and emphasized nature, the natural, the intuition, emotions, and, as far as religion was concerned, mystery and the numinous. 'Seeing the natural world as charged with the supernatural has been seen as the essence of romanticism.'[51]

Frances' delight in alpine scenery, flora and fauna, her detailed descriptions in letters, and her long descriptive poems are typical of the movement (*extracts 14,21*). So was her genuine sense that she could feel closer to God in situations of solitude and natural beauty. Her *Swiss Letters* and also the gift editions of her poems with colour reproductions of paintings of Alpine scenery and flowers were enormously popular and tapped into the ethos of the day.

Frances was a child of her time: unashamedly sentimental. Her letters are sprinkled with underlinings and, for our cynical tastes, too many things are described as 'delicious' or 'nice'. The best of her poems and hymns are timelessly lovely, but the style and subject matter of others were best suited to the nineteenth century. Certainly she used the language of the conventional piety of the time but what she wrote came from her heart — even if sometimes her language is more effusive than is acceptable today. Frances' hymns and poems never descend to the over-sentimentality of some of Sankey's *Sacred Songs and Solos*, which included tear-jerkers such as 'Where is my wandering boy tonight?' or 'Softly and tenderly Jesus is calling' or 'I came to the Garden alone.' This was the age of the music hall, and the popular style was taken up for gospel purposes. Moody and Sankey were enormously effective in reaching the working classes. Frances, ever the musical purist, cringed at some of Sankey's songs, but did accept that if people were being reached for the gospel, then good was being done. She welcomed a visit from Ira Sankey and his wife during the final months of her life. She also admired, and corresponded with, the famous blind American hymnwriter, Frances Jane van Alstyne (Fanny Crosby).

The Keswick Movement

Frances' name became linked with the Keswick Movement, as her hymns became a staple component of the Keswick Convention (an annual meeting of evangelicals in the Lake District, first held in 1875 with the aim of the promotion of 'practical holiness'). Keswick teaching could be summed up as 'sanctification by faith'.[52] This emphasis had been a feature of the annual Mildmay conferences, organized by William Pennefather (a few of which Frances had attended). Many Christians in America had been influenced by the 'holiness' teaching of such as the Pearsall Smiths. Some even advocated that Christians should expect to achieve sinless perfection in this life. In turn 'holiness' teaching became very popular among British evangelicals in the second half of the nineteenth century.[53] Frances never attended Keswick. Her teaching and experience were, she said, the result of private Bible study and prayer, not conferences or conventions. She did not believe that a Christian could ever achieve sinless perfection in this life. Unlike many Keswick leaders, she was not premillennial in her view of the last things, rather holding to one final return of Christ. It would be unfair to associate her with all Keswick teaching, just because her hymns became so popular with convention-goers.

Having said that, her experience and writings perhaps seemed to endorse two of the Keswick emphases.

Firstly, her writings show very little awareness of issues of social or economic justice. Other female writers of the nineteenth century were keenly aware of social injustice: for example Elizabeth Gaskell (*Mary Barton, North and South, Ruth*), or even Charlotte Brontë (*Shirley*). Frances' own privileged background could have been broadened out by the imaginative identity with the underclass provided by the best of Victorian fiction. But she shunned novels. Keswick evangelicalism has been accused of being too individualistic, and not aware enough of wider social issues.

Secondly, Frances enjoyed a one-off and intense spiritual experience (on Advent Sunday, 1873), and then attributed to this experience a change of life: peace replacing worry; perfect assurance replacing insecurity. Arguably the peace and enjoyment which she enjoyed in her last years cannot be separated from her deliberate, careful, obedient discipleship over preceding years — her prayer, meditation, Bible memorization and study, witnessing and worship. The danger of putting her experience in writing was that

Christians who could not be bothered with all of that painful discipline might then attend a Keswick Convention and expect a consecration experience that would lift them onto the same plane of peace and assurance. Keswick teaching could become a short cut for the lazy. Consecration and surrender could be misread as passivity. Frances would not have endorsed the unhealthier extreme of Keswick teaching, but some of her hymns and poems could be hijacked by advocates of that extreme.

In March 1879 (the year of her death) she noted 'H — converted; and O — P — consecrated.' Her sister Maria explained this journal entry as follows:

[Frances] had promised to take most needed rest from her desk-work on the breezy cliffs that afternoon. The hour passed by, and still her door was shut. Then she came, beaming of course: 'Marie, I've had such a tussle with Satan! I had my hat on and was going to the cliffs with you when I saw O. P. on a ladder painting my study windows. I was so tired, that it was quite a battle to talk to him then, but I threw the window open to ask how he was getting on. Directly he said, 'O, Miss Frances, I've been longing for weeks for a chance to speak to you.' Then came such an outpour of his desire to be quite out and out on the Lord's side; so I saw the time was come, as I expected it would from our last conversation. So I told him to come in through the window; and after reading and prayer, I asked if he would now in his own words say to Jesus himself, 'Thou art my King.' And so he did, fully and really, and the answer 'I will be thy King' seemed to fall with

*hushing power as we knelt. And afterwards he
told me how differently he left my study than
when he came in, so glad that Jesus was henceforth his King as well as his Saviour.*[54]

This terminology fits the 'two-tier' emphasis increasingly
adopted by proponents of Keswick teaching, and could
be read in such a way as to encourage the idea that consecration can be reached by a one-off experience. (It
should be noted that in recent years, the teaching at the
Keswick Convention has moved away from the 'higher
life' emphasis, and now represents a broader section of
conservative evangelicalism).

Conclusion

Frances was a woman who lived all out for God. In her
everyday life she wanted to 'bring a blessing' to everyone
she encountered. She wrote her hymns, poems, books
and letters because she wanted to bring that same blessing to a wider audience. With the perspective of hindsight
one can see that the Victorians sometimes overindulged in
sentimentality, the nineteenth-century evangelicals were
sometimes over-serious, the Romantic Movement was
sometimes overblown, and the Keswick movement veered
towards the over-emotional.

Yet the life and writings of Frances Ridley Havergal
represent and express the best elements of Victorian
evangelicalism. She was a child of her times — and she
certainly suffered the limitations placed on single women
during that era. But the struggles she went through resulted
in a deeper dependence upon God, and her transparent
radiance of testimony perhaps speaks even more clearly

today when we are generally so cynical and reticent to show enthusiasm about anything. The theme of her entire life was consecration, perhaps summed up in the single verse:

> *In full and glad surrender we give ourselves to*
>   *Thee,*
> *Thine utterly, and only, and evermore to be!*
> *O Son of God, who lovest us, we will be Thine*
>   *alone,*
> *And all we are, and all we have, shall hence-*
>   *forth be Thine own!*[55]

Selections from her writings

Extract 1: Consecration hymn

This is probably one of the 'top ten' hymns of all time:

'Here we offer and present unto Thee, O Lord, ourselves, our souls and bodies, to be a reasonable, holy and lively sacrifice unto Thee.'

Take my life, and let it be
Consecrated, Lord, to Thee,
Take my moments and my days,
Let them flow in ceaseless praise.

Take my hands and let them move
At the impulse of Thy love;
Take my feet and let them be
Swift and beautiful for Thee.

Take my voice and let me sing
Always, only for my King;

Take my lips and let them be
Filled with messages from Thee.

Take my silver and my gold,
Not a mite would I withhold;
Take my intellect and use
Every power as Thou shalt choose.

Take my will and make it Thine;
It shall be no longer mine:
Take my heart, it is Thine own;
It shall be Thy royal throne.

Take my love; my Lord I pour
At Thy feet its treasure store:
Take myself and I will be
Ever, only, all for Thee![56]

Extract 2: 'What hast thou done for Me?'

In 1858 Frances visited the home of a German pastor and was deeply moved by the words written under a painting of Christ, which read: 'I did this for thee! What hast thou done for me?' Maria writes, 'She had come in weary and sat down opposite a picture with this motto. At once the lines flashed upon her, and she wrote them in pencil on a scrap of paper. Reading them over, they did not satisfy her. She tossed them into the fire, but they fell out untouched. Showing them some months after to her father, he encouraged her to preserve them, and wrote the tune "Baca" especially for them.'[57] Frances matched each line with an appropriate Scripture text as follows:

I gave My life for thee,	Gal. 2:20
My precious blood I shed,	1 Peter 1:19
That thou might'st ransomed be,	Eph. 1:7
And quickened from the dead.	Eph. 2:1
I gave My life for thee;	Titus 2:14
What hast thou given for Me?	John 21:15–17

I spent long years for thee	1 Tim. 1:15
In weariness and woe,	Isa. 53:3
That an eternity	John 17:24
Of joy thou mightest know.	John 16:22
I spent long years for thee;	John 1:10–11
Hast thou spent one for Me?	1 Peter 4:2

My Father's home of light,	John 17:5
My rainbow-circled throne,	Rev. 4:3
I left, for earthly night,	Phil. 2:7
For wanderings sad and lone.	Matt. 7:20
I left it all for thee;	2 Cor. 8:9
Hast thou left aught for Me?	Luke 10:29

I suffered much for thee,	Isa. 53:5
More than thy tongue may tell.	Matt. 26:39
Of bitterest agony,	Luke 22:44
To rescue thee from hell.	Rom. 5:9
I suffered much for thee;	1 Peter 2:21–24
What canst thou bear for Me?	Rom. 8:17–18

And I have brought to thee,	John 4:10,14
Down from My home above,	John 3:13
Salvation full and free,	Rev. 21:6
My pardon and My love.	Acts 5:31
Great gifts I brought to thee;	Ps. 68:18
What hast thou brought to Me?	Rom. 7:1

Oh, let thy life be given,	Rom. 6:13
Thy years for Me be spent,	2 Cor. 5:15
World-fetters all be riven,	Phil. 3:8
And joy with suffering blent;	1 Peter 4:13–16
I gave Myself to thee:	Eph. 5:2
Give thou thyself to Me!	Prov. 23:28[58]

Extract 3: 'Lord, speak to me'

This hymn, written while staying at Winterdyne in April 1872, can be read as the prayer that Frances prayed daily for her own life.

Lord, speak to me, that I may speak
In living echoes of Thy tone;
As Thou hast sought, so let me seek
Thy erring children lost and lone.

O lead me, Lord, that I may lead
The wandering and the wavering feet;
O feed me, Lord, that I may feed
Thy hungering ones with manna sweet.

O strengthen me, that, while I stand
Firm on the rock, and strong in Thee,
I may stretch out a loving hand
To wrestlers with the troubled sea.

O teach me, Lord, that I may teach
The precious things Thou dost impart;
And wing my words, that they may reach
The hidden depths of many a heart.

O give Thine own sweet rest to me,
That I may speak with soothing power
A word in season, as from Thee,
To weary ones in needful hour.

O fill me with Thy fulness, Lord,
Until my very heart o'erflow
In kindling thought and glowing word,
Thy love to tell, Thy praise to show.

O use me, Lord, use even me,
Just as Thou wilt and when, and where,
Until Thy blessed face I see,
Thy rest, Thy joy, Thy glory share.[59]

Extract 4: 'Who is on the Lord's side?'

This hymn encapsulates the evangelical 'world-view'. Humanity is divided into two sides: those for God and those for the world. Those who are for God will, by definition, be against the world. Frances unashamedly uses military imagery throughout this battle cry, which is a rebuke to the lukewarm and lazy.

Who is on the Lord's side?
Who will serve the King?
Who will be His helpers
Other lives to bring?
Who will leave the world's side?
Who will face the foe?
Who is on the Lord's side?
Who for him will go?
By Thy call of mercy,

By Thy grace divine,
We are on the Lord's side;
Saviour we are Thine.

Jesus, Thou hast bought us,
Not with gold or gem,
But with Thine own life-blood,
For Thy diadem.
With Thy blessing filling
Each who comes to Thee,
Thou hast made us willing,
Thou hast made us free.
By Thy great redemption,
By Thy grace divine,
We are on the Lord's side;
Saviour we are Thine.

Fierce may be the conflict,
Strong may be the foe;
But the King's own army
None can overthrow.
Round his standard ranging,
Victory is secure;
For his truth unchanging
Makes the triumph sure.
Joyfully enlisting,
By Thy grace divine,
We are on the Lord's side;
Saviour we are Thine.

Chosen to be soldiers
In an alien land,
Chosen, called and faithful,

For our Captain's band,
In the service royal
Let us not grow cold;
Let us be right loyal,
Noble, true, and bold.
Master, Thou wilt keep us,
By Thy grace divine,
Always on the Lord's side,
Saviour, always Thine.[60]

Extract 5: 'Master, say on!'

The theme of consecration runs through a very large number of poems. The well known hymn 'Master, speak! Thy servant heareth' is taken from a longer poem, written as a personal prayer. Frances wrote it while in Weston-super-Mare, on Sunday evening 19 May 1867, hence the reference to the 'moonrise o'er the bay' in verse 2.

Master, speak! Thy servant heareth,
Waiting for Thy gracious word,
Longing for Thy voice that cheereth;
Master! let it now be heard.
I am listening, Lord, for Thee;
What hast Thou to say to me?

Master, speak in love and power:
Crown the mercies of the day,
In this quiet evening hour
Of the moonrise o'er the bay,
With the music of Thy voice;
Speak! and bid Thy child rejoice.

Often through my heart is pealing
Many another voice than Thine,
Many an unwilled echo stealing
From the walls of this Thy shrine:
Let Thy longed-for accents fall;
Master, speak! and silence all.

Master, speak! I do not doubt Thee,
Though so tearfully I plead;
Saviour, Shepherd! oh, without Thee
Life would be a blank indeed!
But I long for fuller light,
Deeper love and clearer sight.

Resting on the 'faithful saying',
Trusting what Thy gospel saith,
On Thy written promise staying
All my hope in life and death,
Yet I long for something more
From Thy love's exhaustless store.

Speak to me by name, O Master,
Let me know it is to me;
Speak, that I may follow faster,
With a step more firm and free,
Where the Shepherd leads the flock,
In the shadow of the Rock.

Master, speak! I kneel before Thee,
Listening, longing, waiting still;
Oh, how long shall I implore Thee
This petition to fulfil?
Hast Thou not one word for me?
Must my prayer unanswered be?

Master, speak! though least and lowest,
Let me not unheard depart;
Master, speak! For oh, Thou knowest
All the yearning of my heart,
Knowest all its truest need;
Speak! and make me blest indeed.

Master, speak! and make me ready,
When Thy voice is truly heard
With obedience glad and steady
Still to follow every word.
I am listening, Lord, for Thee;
Master, speak, oh, speak to me![61]

Extract 6: 'Tell it out!'

This stirring missionary hymn was written at Winterdyne, on Sunday, 21 April 1872. Frances was ill, and unable to attend church, so she followed the service for the day in her Prayer Book. When she reached Psalm 96:10 ('Tell it out among the heathen that the Lord is King') the 'words and music came rushing in to me' and she went down to the piano to work it out. When the others came back from church, the words, music and harmonies were all written out 'with copperplate neatness'.

Frances had at one time hoped to volunteer for overseas mission; when disappointed in this ambition she became a tireless advocate of, and collector for, the cause, and she threw herself into 'home missions' when she had opportunity. This hymn expresses her heart for mission. For use today, 'nations' could be substituted for 'heathen' throughout.

*Tell it out among the heathen that the Lord is
King!
Tell it out, tell it out!
Tell it out among the nations, bid them shout
and sing!
Tell it out, tell it out!
Tell it out with adoration, that He shall increase;
That the mighty King of Glory is the King of
Peace.
Tell it out with jubilation, though the waves
may roar,
That He sitteth on the water-floods, our King
for evermore!
Tell it out!*

*Tell it out among the nations that the Saviour
reigns!
Tell it out, tell it out!
Tell it out among the heathen, bid them burst
their chains!
Tell it out, tell it out!
Tell it out among the weeping ones that Jesus
lives;
Tell it out among the weary ones what rest He
gives;
Tell it out among the sinners that He came to
save;
Tell it out among the dying that He triumphed
o'er the grave.
Tell it out!*

*Tell it out among the nations Jesus reigns
    above!
Tell it out, tell it out!
Tell it out among the heathen that His name
    is Love!
Tell it out, tell it out!
Tell it out among the highways and the lanes
    at home;
Let it ring across the mountains and the ocean
    foam;
Like the sound of many waters let our glad
    shout be,
Till it echo and re-echo from the islands of the
    sea!
Tell it out!*[62]

Extract 7: 'Chosen in Christ'

Later nineteenth-century evangelicalism has been criticized
for being overly individualistic, focusing on private religious
experience. Frances Havergal emphasized the importance of the church. While many would stress an individualistic interpretation of Ephesians 1:4, here she shows
that election is a truth applied to the whole body of Christ,
not just the individual believer.

*He hath chosen us in Him before the foundation of the
world (Ephesians 1:4, KJV):*

> *O thou chosen Church of Jesus, glorious
>   blessed and secure,
> Founded on the One Foundation, which for
>   ever shall endure;*

*Not thy holiness or beauty can thy strength
and safety be,
But the everlasting love wherewith Jehovah
loveth thee.*

*Chosen — by His own good pleasure, by the
counsel of His will,
Mystery of power and wisdom working for His
people still;
Chosen — in thy mighty Saviour, ere one ray
of quickening light
Beamed upon the chaos, waiting for the Word
of sovereign might.*

*Chosen — through the Holy Spirit, through
the sanctifying grace
Poured upon his precious vessels, meetened
for the heavenly place;
Chosen — to show forth His praises, to be
holy in His sight;
Chosen — unto grace and glory, chosen unto
life and light.*

*Blessed be the God and Father of our Saviour
Jesus Christ,
Who hath blessed us with such blessings all
uncounted and unpriced!
Let our high and holy calling, and our strong
salvation be,
Theme of never-ending praises, God of sover-
eign grace to Thee!*[63]

Extract 8: 'I am trusting'

This was Frances Havergal's personal favourite, written in September 1874. Its simplicity makes it timeless.

I am trusting Thee, Lord Jesus,
Trusting only Thee;
Trusting Thee for full salvation
Great and free.

I am trusting Thee for pardon;
At Thy feet I bow,
For Thy grace and tender mercy,
Trusting now.

I am trusting Thee for cleansing,
In the crimson flood;
Trusting Thee to make me holy
By Thy blood.

I am trusting Thee to guide me;
Thou alone shalt lead,
Every day and hour supplying
All my need.

I am trusting Thee for power;
Thine can never fail;
Words which Thou Thyself shalt give me,
Must prevail.

I am trusting Thee, Lord Jesus:
Never let me fall;
I am trusting Thee for ever
And for all.[64]

Extract 9: 'Thou art coming'

This magnificent hymn was written originally for the communion service, which is to be celebrated 'until he comes'.

Thou art coming, O my Saviour!
Thou art coming, O my King!
In Thy beauty all-resplendent,
In Thy glory all-transcendent;
Well may we rejoice and sing!
Coming! In the opening east,
Herald brightness slowly swells;
Coming! O my glorious Priest:
Hear we not Thy golden bells?

Thou art coming! At Thy table
We are witnesses for this;
While remembering hearts Thou meetest,
In communion, clearest, sweetest,
Earnest of our coming bliss.
Showing not Thy death alone,
And Thy love exceeding great,
But Thy coming and Thy throne,
All for which we long and wait.

O the joy to see Thee reigning,
Thee, my own beloved Lord;
Every tongue Thy name confessing —
Worship, honour, glory, blessing,
Brought to Thee with one accord!
Thee, my Master and my Friend,
Vindicated and enthroned!
Unto earth's remotest end
Glorified, adored and owned![65]

Extract 10: 'Whose I am'
and 'Whom I serve'

Written in December 1865, these four verses are taken from the two poems 'Whose I am' and 'Whom I serve', each of which has three stanzas.

Jesus, Master, whose I am,
Purchased Thine alone to be,
By Thy blood, O spotless Lamb,
Shed so willingly for me:
Let my heart be all Thine own,
Let me live to Thee alone.

Jesus, Master, whom I serve,
Though so feebly and so ill,
Strengthen hand and heart and nerve
All Thy bidding to fulfil:
Open now mine eyes to see
All the work Thou hast for me.

Jesus, Master! wilt Thou use
One who owes Thee more than all?
As Thou wilt! I would not choose;
Only let me hear Thy call.
Jesus! let me always be
In Thy service, glad and free.

Jesus, Master, I am Thine;
Keep me faithful, keep me near;
Let Thy presence in me shine
All my homeward way to cheer.
Jesus! at Thy feet I fall;
Oh be Thou my All-in-all.[66]

Extract 11: 'I could not do
without Thee'

Written 7 May 1873, this hymn reflects the absolute
dependence on God that Frances experienced and the
comfort and completeness she found in her Saviour.

I could not do without Thee,
O Saviour of the lost!
Whose precious blood redeemed me,
At such tremendous cost.
Thy righteousness, Thy pardon,
Thy precious blood must be
My only hope and comfort,
My glory and my plea!

I could not do without Thee!
I cannot stand alone,
I have no strength or goodness,
No wisdom of my own.
But Thou, beloved Saviour,
Art all in all to me;
And weakness will be power,
If leaning hard on Thee.

I could not do without Thee!
No other friend can read
The spirit's strange deep longings,
Interpreting its need.
No human heart could enter
Each dim recess of mine,
And sooth and hush and calm it,
O blessed Lord, but Thine![67]

Extract 12: Perfect peace

This beautiful hymn is a favourite with many. Frances composed it in Leamington, during a severe illness. She dictated it while lying in bed.

Like a river glorious
Is God's perfect peace,
Over all victorious,
In its bright increase:
Perfect — yet it floweth
Fuller every day;
Perfect, yet it groweth
Deeper all the way.

Stayed upon Jehovah,
Hearts are fully blessed,
Finding as He promised,
Perfect peace and rest.

Hidden in the hollow
Of His blessed hand,
Never foe can follow,
Never traitor stand.
Not a surge of worry,
Not a shade of care,
Not a blast of hurry
Touch the spirit there.

Every joy or trial,
Falleth from above,
Traced upon our dial
By the Sun of Love.

We may trust him solely
All for us to do;
They who trust him wholly,
Find him wholly true. [68]

Extract 13: 'My Master'

Exodus 21:1–6 outlines a law whereby a Hebrew slave had to be offered freedom in the seventh year of service. But if the slave 'plainly says I love my master, my wife and my children, I will not go out free', then he could choose to stay with his master 'for ever' — the permanence of the arrangement symbolized by the master's boring through the slave's ear with an awl. Frances loved the picture of voluntarily choosing to serve Christ for ever. While in Fins Haut in July 1876 she wrote a nine-verse poem on the theme, of which four verses follow:

I love, I love my Master,
I will not go out free,
For He is my Redeemer,
He paid the price for me.

I would not halve my service,
His only it must be, —
His only who so loved me
And gave himself for me.

He chose me for His service,
And gave me power to choose
That blessed, 'perfect freedom'
Which I shall never lose.

Rejoicing and adoring,
Henceforth my song shall be:
I love, I love my Master,
I will not go out free! [69]

Extract 14: The thoughts of God

The poem 'Thoughts of God' appears in the *Oxford Book of Mystical Verse* — a massive twenty-six-stanza rendering of Psalm 139, culminating in a poetic treatment of verse 17, 'How precious to me are your thoughts O God! How vast is the sum of them', in which Frances shows that God reveals his thoughts in creation, providence his Word, and salvation. The first and final verses are as follows:

Thy thoughts, O God! O theme Divine!
Except Thy Spirit in my darkness shine,
And make it light,
And overshadow me
With stilling might,
And touch my lips that I may speak of Thee, —
How shall I soar
To thoughts of Thy thoughts? And how dare to
 write
Of Thine?

They say there is a hollow, safe and still,
A point of coolness and repose
Within the centre of a flame, where life might
 dwell
Unharmed and unconsumed, as in a luminous
 shell,

Which the bright walls of fire enclose
In breachless splendour, barrier that no foes
Could pass at will.

There is a point of rest
At the great centre of the cyclone's force,
A silence at its secret source; —
A little child might slumber undistressed,
Without the ruffle of one fairy curl,
In that strange central calm amid the mighty
  whirl.

So, in the centre of these thoughts of God,
Cyclones of power, consuming glory-fire, —
As we fall o'erawed
Upon our faces, and are lifted higher
By His great gentleness, and carried nigher
Than unredeemed angels, till we stand
Even in the hollow of His hand, —
Nay, more! We lean upon His breast —
There, there we find a point of perfect rest
And glorious safety. There we see
His thoughts to usward, thoughts of peace
That stoop in tenderest love; that still increase
With increase of our need; that never change,
That never fail, or falter, or forget.
O pity infinite!
O royal mercy free!
O gentle climax of the depth and height
Of God's most precious thoughts, most
  wonderful, most strange!
'For I am poor and needy, yet
The Lord Himself, Jehovah, thinketh upon me!'[70]

Extract 15: Kept for the Master's use

Frances wrote a book entitled *Kept for the Master's Use* to accompany the hymn 'Take my life'. She used the word 'keep' rather than 'take' throughout. 'He who is able and willing to take unto himself is no less able and willing to keep for himself.' She wrote a chapter on each line giving biblical references and practical applications. The concluding chapter traces how Jesus Christ has given all for us: his life, his time, his hands, his feet, his voice, his lips, his wealth, his wisdom, his will, his heart, his love, himself. Part of that final chapter runs as follows:

> *His life for thee.* 'The Good Shepherd gives his life for the sheep.' Oh, wonderful gift! not promised but given; not to friends but to enemies. Given without condition, without reserve, without return. Himself unknown and unloved, his gift unsought and unasked, he gave his life for thee; a more than royal bounty — the greatest gift that Deity could devise. Oh, grandeur of love! 'I lay down my life for the sheep.' And we for whom he gave it have held back, and hesitated to give our lives, not even for him (he has not asked us to do that) but to him. But that is past and he has tenderly pardoned the unloving, ungrateful reserve and has graciously accepted the poor little fleeting breath and speck of dust which was all we had to offer. And now his precious death and his glorious life are all 'for thee'.
>
> *His eternity for thee.* All we can ask him to take are days and moments — the little span given us as it is given, and of this only the present in

deed and the future in will. As for the past in so far as we did not give it to him it is too late; we can never give it now. But his past was given to us, though ours was not given to him. Oh, what a tremendous debt does this show us!

Away back in the dim depths of past eternity, 'or ever the earth and the world were made', his divine existence in the bosom of his Father was all for thee, purposing and planning for thee, receiving and holding the promise of eternal life for thee.

Then the thirty-three years among sinners on this sinful earth: do we think enough of the slow-wearing days and nights, the heavy-footed hours, the never-hastening minutes, that went to make up those thirty-three years of trial and humiliation? We all know how slowly time passes when suffering and sorrow are near, and there is no reason to suppose that our Master was exempted from this part of our infirmities.

Then his present is for thee. Even now he liveth to make intercession; even now he 'thinketh upon me'; even now he 'knoweth', he 'careth', he 'loveth'.

Then, only to think that his whole eternity will be 'for thee'. Millions of ages of unfoldings of all his love and of ever new declarings of his Father's name to his brethren. Think of it! and can we ever hesitate to give all our poor little hours to his service?

His love for thee. Not a passive, possible love but outflowing, yes outpouring of the real, glowing, personal love of his mighty and tender *heart. Love, not as an attribute, a quality, a latent force but an acting, moving, reaching, touching, and grasping power. Love, not a cold, beautiful, far-off star but a sunshine that comes and enfolds us, making us warm and glad and strong and bright and fruitful.*

His love! What manner of love is it? What should be quoted to prove or describe it? First the whole Bible with its mysteries and marvels of redemption, then the whole book of Providence and the whole volume of creation. Then add to these the unknown records of eternity past and the unknown glories of eternity to come, and then let the immeasurable quotation be sung by angels and archangels, and all the company of heaven, with all the harps of God, and still that love will be untold, still it will be 'the love of Christ that passes knowledge'.

But it is for thee!

Himself for thee. 'Christ also hath loved us, and given himself for us.' 'The Son of God ... loved me, and gave himself for me.' Yes, himself! What is the Bride's true and central treasure? What calls forth the deepest, brightest, sweetest thrill of love and praise? Not the Bridegroom's priceless gifts, not the robe of his resplendent righteousness, not the dowry of unsearchable riches, not the magnificence of the palace home to which he is bringing her, not the glory which she shall share with him, but himself Jesus Christ, 'who his own self bare our sins in his own body on the tree'; this same Jesus, 'whom having not seen, ye love'; the Son of God and

*the Man of Sorrows; my Saviour, my Friend, my
Master, my King, my Priest, my Lord, and my
God — he says, 'I also for thee.' What an 'I'!
What power and sweetness we feel in it, so
different from any human I for all his Godhead
and all his manhood are concentrated in it —
and all for thee.*

*And not only all but ever for thee! His
unchangeableness is the seal upon every
attribute; he will be this same Jesus forever.
How can mortal mind estimate this enormous
promise? How can mortal heart conceive what is
enfolded in these words, 'I also for thee'?*

*One glimpse of its fullness and glory, and we
feel that henceforth it must be, shall be, and by
this grace will be our true-hearted, whole-hearted
cry —*

*Take myself, and I will be
Ever, only, all for thee!*[71]

Extract 16: The perpetual presence

This devotion from her book of daily devotions, *Royal
Bounty* makes it clear that the truth of Christ's promise
does not depend on our feelings on any given day.

*Matthew 28:20: 'Lo, I am with you alway.'
Some of us think and say a good deal about
a sense of his presence; sometimes rejoicing in
it, sometimes going mourning all the day long
(Ps. 38:6) because we have it not (Job 23:3);
praying for it and not always seeming to receive*

what we ask; measuring our own position and sometimes even that of others by it; now on the heights, now in the depths about it. And all this April-like gleam and gloom instead of steady summer glow because we are turning our attention upon the sense of his presence instead of the changeless reality of it!

All our trouble and disappointment about it is met by his own simple word (Heb. 13:5) and vanishes in the simple faith that grasps it. For if Jesus says simply and absolutely, 'Lo, I am with you alway,' what have we to do with feeling or sense about it? We have only to believe it and to recollect it. And it is only by thus believing and recollecting that we can realize it.

It comes practically to this: Are you a disciple of the Lord Jesus at all? If so, he says to you, 'I am with you alway.' That overflows all the regrets of the past and all the possibilities of the future and most certainly includes the present (Exod. 3:12). Therefore, at this very moment, as surely as your eyes rest on this page so surely is the Lord Jesus with you. 'I am,' is neither 'I was' nor 'I will be.' It is always abreast of our lives, always encompassing us with salvation. It is a splendid perpetual now. It always means 'I am with you now' or it would cease to be 'I am' and 'always.' (Acts 18:9–10)[72]

Extract 17: Little Pillows

Frances wrote several devotional books for children. We give the introduction to *Little Pillows* (in which she explains how it came to be written during the visit of one of her nieces), and then the first of the devotions in that book:

> *A little girl was away from home on a week's visit. We will suppose her name was Amy.*[73] *The first night, when she was tucked up in bed, and just ready for a good-night kiss, I said, 'Now, shall I give you a little pillow?'*
>
> *Amy lifted her head to see what was under it, and said, 'I have got one, Auntie!'*
>
> *'It was another sort of pillow that I meant to give you; I wonder if you will like it?'*
>
> *So then, Amy saw it was not a question of feathers and pillow-case; still she did not understand, and so she laughed and said, 'Do tell me at once, Auntie, what you mean; don't keep me waiting to guess!'*
>
> *Then I told her that, just as we wanted a nice soft pillow to lay our heads down upon at night, our hearts wanted a pillow too, something to rest upon, some word that we might go to sleep upon happily and peacefully. And that it was a good plan to take a little text for our pillow every night. So she had one that night, and the next night.*
>
> *The third night I was prevented from coming up till long after Amy should have been asleep. But there were the bright eyes peeping out robin-redbreast fashion, and a reproachful little voice said, 'Auntie, you have not given me any little pillow tonight!'*
>
> *'Then, do you really care about having the little pillows given you, Amy?'*

'Oh, of course I do!' was the answer. She did not seem to think there could possibly be any doubt about it!

So it seemed that perhaps other little ones would like to have 'little pillows' put ready for every night. For even little hearts are sometimes very weary, and want something to rest upon; and a happy little heart, happy in the love of Jesus, will always be glad to have one of his own words to go to sleep upon.

So here are thirty-one 'little pillows', not to be used all at once, nor even two at a time, but one for every night in the month. The little texts are so short, that they will need no learning; but when you have read the explanation you will be able to keep the text quite safely and quite easily in your mind.

Read the little book before you kneel down to say your evening prayers, because I hope what you read will always remind you of something to pray about. And then, when you lie down and shut your eyes, let your heart rest upon the 'little pillow' until 'He giveth His beloved sleep'.

First Day: The Invitation. 'Come unto me'
(Matthew 11:28)
What kind words for your pillow tonight! Jesus says them to you.

'How am I to know?' Well, they are for everyone that is weary and heavy laden. Do not you know what it is to be weary and tired sometimes? Perhaps you know what it is to feel almost tired of trying to be good — weary with

wishing you could be better. So you see, it is to you that He says, 'Come!'

And if you have not yet come, you are heavy laden too, even if you do not feel it; because the burden of sin is heavy enough to sink you down into hell, unless Jesus takes it from you. So it is to you that He says 'Come!'

And lest you think He says it to grown-up people only, He said 'Suffer the little children to come unto me.' Are you a little child? Then it is to you that He says 'Come!'

'If He were here and I could see Him, I should like to come.' He is here, as really and truly as you are. Suppose your mother and you were in a dark room together, and she said 'Come to me!' you would not stop to say, 'I would come if I could see you.' You would say, 'I am coming, mother!' and you would soon feel your way across the room, and be safe by her side. Not seeing her would not make any difference.

Jesus calls you now, this very night. He is here, in this very room. Now, will you not say, 'I am coming, Lord Jesus!' and ask Him to stretch out His hand and help you to come, and draw you quite close to himself?

Yes, to Himself, the blessed, beloved Lord Jesus, who loved you and gave himself for you, who has waited so patiently for you, who calls you because He wants you to come and be his own little lamb, and be taken up into His arms and blessed. Will you keep Him waiting any longer? Will you not 'come'?[74]

Extract 18: Pastoral letters

Frances conducted a voluminous correspondence. By the end of her life she was receiving, on average, 600 letters a week. She spent a great deal of time and care giving one-to-one spiritual encouragement and advice, and was willing to risk friendships when she thought that a word of correction was called for, as in the following letter:

MY DEAR —,   *Tuesday, 7 a.m.*
As I have already had one bad night, and several troubled wakings, all about you, I had better get it off my mind. I write to you as one who is really wanting to follow Jesus altogether, really wanting to live and speak EXACTLY according to His commands and His beautiful example; and when this is the standard, what seems a little thing, or nothing at all, to others, is seen to be sin, because it is disobeying His dear word and not 'following fully.' 'Whatsoever ye would that men should do unto you, do ye even so to them.'
Now, darling, be true to yourself, and to Him, as to these His own words. Would you like any one to retell, and dwell upon, little incidents which made you appear weak, tiresome, capricious, foolish? Yet, dear, everything which we say of another which we would not like them to say of us (unless said with some right and pure object which Jesus Himself would approve), is transgression of this distinct command of our dear Lord's, and therefore sin, — sin which needs nothing less than His blood to cleanse, sin in which we indulge at our peril and to the certain

244 In trouble and in joy

detriment of our spiritual life. And Jesus hears
every word, and sees, to the depth, the want of
real conformity to His own loving spirit, from
which they spring. Do not think I am condemning
you without seeing my own failures. It is just
because it is a special battle-field of my own that
I am the more pained and quick to feel it, when
others, who love Jesus, yield to the temptation
or do not see it to be temptation. I know the
temptation it is to allow oneself to say things
which one would not say if the person were
present, yes, and if Jesus were visibly present.
And I have seen and felt how even a momentary
indulgence in the mildest forms of 'speaking
evil,' which is so absolutely forbidden, injures
one's own soul, and totally prevents clear,
unclouded communion with Jesus. So I want
you to recognise and shun and resolutely and
totally 'put away' this thing.

I should not write all this but that I long for
your eyes to be opened to the principle, for
other's sakes, for your own soul's sake, and for
Christ's sake. I want you to pray over it, to search
bravely to the bottom, and to put it all into the
hands of Jesus, that He may not only forgive but
cleanse, and so fill you with His love that it (and
nothing else) may overflow into all your words,
that He may 'make you to increase and abound
in love ... to the end He may establish your heart
unblameable in holiness.' Oh, if you knew how I
pray for this for myself, you would not wonder at
my anxiety about it for you and for others! So
don't be vexed with, yours ever lovingly...[75]

Extract 19: One-to-one ministry

This extract gives just one example of Frances' deep concern for individuals. She always felt that her prime ministry was conducted on a one-to-one level. This incident happened in 1864 when she was visiting her father in Shareshill.

Hannah and Janey and Andrienne V. were coming for a visit. A special impulse seemed to come upon me to pray for H., and that her visit might be blessed. She came to Shareshill reluctantly, and with a special determination not to like me, and inclination to be jealous of me. She baffled me, and knew it; no response whatever could I get. I think God poured out upon me the spirit of grace and of supplication for her, so much so that I almost lost sight of my own difficulties and depression in anxiety for her. July 2nd, Saturday evening, she broke the ice, by merely saying, 'You are what I am not.' 'Then why not?' This led to a very serious talk the next evening; and she cried, but said, 'I just feel that I don't care enough about it to be worth while to seek.' I spoke of danger and of God's promise to give the Holy Spirit to them that only ask. All through the following week, she sought truly and earnestly. By Maria's advice, though reluctantly at first, I read a little with her each day, and soon was most thankful that I had been led to do so. On Saturday, 9th, I gave her Mark 10:46–52, and the first light seemed to break in. That evening we sat on the stile behind the churchyard close to our gardens; we read

Rom. 3, dwelling long on verse 22 and the doctrine of imputed righteousness. And God gave her faith to receive it; — 'I do believe this, but is that all? Can it be all? is nothing more necessary?' I assured her it must be all, because God had said it. 'Isn't it too good to be true?' was the next. But she believed the testimony concerning His Son, and was at rest. And the next day, July 11th, she sealed her faith in obedience to her Saviour's command, and came with us for the first time in her life to His table.[76]

Extract 20: YMCA classes

It is very dangerous to pass judgement on accounts of what happens during times of renewal — genuine expressions of contrition may be misconstrued as emotionalism. An account of one of her YWCA classes shows that Frances was unabashed about emotional expressions of repentance.

My Friday evening class is specially blessed. I now have 24 young women ... many walk from long distances. Last Friday ... I broke off my lesson in the middle, and made it a heart to heart personal 'now or perhaps never' appeal. I never in all my life so felt Christ's actual presence with us, nor saw such intense, perfectly breathless attention; nearly all were in tears. Then I asked all who really wanted to close with Christ's offer of salvation then and there to stay with me. Eleven stayed. I asked them to kneel and remain kneeling, and then I prayed for and with them — not continuously but with intervals of silence, leaving them with Jesus. Then I went softly round to everyone, so softly as not to disturb even the one kneeling next, asking my Master to give me the right word for each. Reserve seemed broken; everyone, even the shyest, whispered freely what they felt; four found Him then and there with perfect joy and freedom; four more seemed no less really to have come to Him only did not speak quite so strongly; two who had come before were filled with quite new peace and conscious nearness, and only one of the eleven went away unsatisfied ... yet ... her desires were greatly intensified to find Jesus. Of those whom either shyness or promise to be home prevented from remaining, I have not yet seen all; but ... not one seems 'left out.' Two or three 'went out and wept bitterly' for sin; one, 'never saw what a sinner she was before.' Another has written most touchingly to me, another went home to pray for the very first time.[77]

Extract 21: Swiss Letters

Frances spent June and July 1869 in Europe with her elder sister Jane Crane, her brother-in-law Henry (HC in her letters) and their daughter, Miriam Louisa (ML or M in her letters). Each evening she sat down to write to her family at home about what they had done that day: the letters circulated between her sisters Maria and Ellen and her brother Frank. Most of us find it hard enough on holiday to scribble a few postcards — the entry below is typical of the length of the letter written each day!

*June 15, 1869 — INTERLACHEN TO
LAUTERBRUNNEN*

*After rain, sunshine; so we set off at four in
an open carriage to Lauterbrunnen in a perfectly
transparent atmosphere. Fancy nine miles drive
up a deep valley, hills six or seven thousand feet
high on each side, wooded wherever trees could
get root, and where not, rocky and precipitous,
between them at each opening views of snow
mountains glittering in brilliant light; below, a
wild stream, the Lutschine, rushing in one perpetual downhill of rapids and little falls; every
now and then a silver thread of a waterfall
gleaming out on the farther side of the valley,
or a broad riband of one dashing down the
nearer side to our very feet, to be crossed by a
little bridge, then the whole picture 'grounded'
with all shades of the freshest, brightest green,
still wet with the morning's rain and canopied
with vivid blue. And at every turn coming nearer
to the Jungfrau, 'Queen of the Alps', which fills
up the valley in front, and only hides herself
again when we get too close under her silver
throne! Was not this 'something like'?*

*It struck me again here, as in Scotland last
summer, what marvellous lavishment of beauty
God has poured upon the details of His works.
For here, in the presence of these culminations
of earthly magnificence, scenes beyond what we
ever saw before, if the eye dropped and rested
on the very ground it was just as beautiful in its
proportion as if there were no other loveliness
for us far or near; ferns, and flowers, and grasses,*

and mossy boulders, and tiny streams, every square foot being a little world of beauty. One item in these minor charms was the luxuriant way in which the firs had sown themselves, thousands of wee fir trees springing up on banks and among rocks, some standing alone in green tiny gracefulness, others growing in the prettiest little miniature groves you can imagine. I never saw firs growing this way anywhere else; they were like kittens to cats, so very pretty and petable.

Near Lauterbrunnen we passed under tremendous bastions of rock as the gorge narrowed in; and then saw the long waving veil of delicate white mist, and needed no telling that it was the Staubbach. We walked on to its foot, and H. C. irreverently suggested what a first rate shower bath it would be! I should not mind trying, it comes down so temptingly and fairily, not nearly so substantially as in its picture. We walked a mile or more up the valley, enjoying the evening sunshine on the Jungfrau, and its shining and most pure Silberhorn and other white peaks before us. And just as we returned, and the valley was darkening, lo the afterglow, which I so much wished to see. Rosy gold, or golden rosiness, comes as near as I can give it; but words of any sort are not much use. One more effect was still in reserve: when we came up to our room, the crescent moon was shedding a pale holy glimmer over the snow, and the sky behind it was no invisible purple or neutral tint, but a most ethereal blue, which I never saw at night before and do not understand.[78]

Extract 22: Gospel opportunities

During a three-day hike in Switzerland on her own in 1874, Frances had to stop one night in a village with only one *auberge*. The hostile reception and appalling service she received was taken as a gospel opportunity:

For the first and only time in Switzerland I found a strange contrast to the civility and even kindness of the people... A tall, rough girl of twenty-five or so let me in. 'Yes, you can have a room when it's ready, not before. Here, in here!' And she ushered me into a dirty room with tables and benches, marched off and shut the door. I did not like my quarters at all, but there was no help for it... It got quite dark, and then five or six men came in, and she brought a candle, and they sat at one of the tables and smoked... I asked if my room was ready. 'No you must wait!' and out she darted, slamming the door. So I waited, sitting on my bench in my dark corner for nearly an hour, she coming roughly in and out, talking noisily and bringing wine for the men. At last! 'You can come upstairs now!'... It was not quite so dirty as downstairs but not brilliant. A jug and basin on the table was all the apparatus, the bed was barley straw, no pillow, but a pink cotton bolster. 'Are you going to bed now?' she asked. I told her yes, very soon. About eight o'clock, just as I really was going to bed, came a sharp angry rap at my door. I was glad it was locked, for before I could answer the handle was rattled violently. 'What

*is it?' 'Are you going to burn the candle all
night? how soon are you going to put it out, I
should like to know! burning it all away comme
cela!' I considered it advisable to answer very
meekly, so I merely said it should be put out in
a few minutes, whereupon she banged downstairs... I asked God that when morning came
he would shut her mouth and open mine...
[next morning at breakfast] I asked her to get
me some coffee. 'Can't have coffee till it's
made' she said savagely. So I went outside the
door and sat patiently. In about half an hour
she poked her head out. 'Do you want anything
beside coffee?' still in a tone as if I were a mortal
enemy! I suggested bread and butter. 'Butter!'
(as if I had asked for turtle soup) 'there is none,
but you can have a piece of bread if you like.'...
Then it was my turn. I went close to her, looked up
into her wicked looking eyes, and said (as gently
as possible) 'You are not happy, I know you are
not.' She darted the oddest look at me; a sort of
startled, half frightened look, as if she thought I
was a witch! I saw I had touched the right string
and followed it up ... and then, finding she was
completely tamed, spoke to her quite plainly and
solemnly about Jesus... She made a desperate
effort not to cry. She listened ... and took* A
Saviour for you *(in French), promising to read it
and thanking me over and over again ... was it
not worth getting out of the groove of one's
usual comforts and civilities?*[79]

Conclusion

They had different personalities and varied situations, but each of these four women lived focused lives, wanting to praise God through days of trouble as well as days of joy. As is true of many women, they had to juggle all sorts of responsibilities. Pursuing holiness did not mean running away from these responsibilities: it involved living every day wholeheartedly for God. In conclusion, we note four aspects of their spirituality that run through their lives and writings.

Submission

Each of these four women shared the conviction that God is totally sovereign, and in control of every aspect of their lives. They believed that if God gives, he also has the right to take away. Emotionally devastated when Richard Baxter moved away to London, Margaret wrote:

> *The will of the Lord be done, for he is wise and*
> *good: we are his own, let him do with us what*

he pleaseth: all shall be for good to them that love God.[1]

Even more moving was Sarah Edwards' magnificent response to the death of her beloved husband:

> *The Lord has done it. He has made me adore his goodness that we had him [her husband] so long. But my God lives; and he has my heart.*[2]

Anne Steele expressed her submission to the will of God in this hymn:

> *What'er thy providence denies*
> *I calmly would resign,*
> *For thou art just and good and wise;*
> *O bend my will to thine!*[3]

Frances Ridley Havergal found peace in submitting to the providence of God in the difficulties of her family situation, in ill health, and also with regard to remaining unmarried. She wrote to a friend who was struggling with singleness:

> *Ask the Lord if it is not his will you should marry to make you perfectly content, and then to take away all the wish out of your heart, so that you may be 'free to serve' with your whole mind undistracted by it. And then ask Him, in His great kindness that He would interpose in some way to make this easy to you, He has such wonderful ways!*[4]

Obedience

In their pursuit of holiness, each of these women believed that obedience to God's commands was not optional: it was a necessity. Like many Puritans, Margaret Baxter wrote her own resolutions, which expressed her desire to obey God completely. Her zeal could lead to anxiety, and her husband found her perfectionism somewhat wearing:

> *She was very desirous that we should all have lived in a constancy of devotion, and a blameless innocency. And, in this respect, she was the meetest helper that I could have had in the world ... for I was apt to be over careless in my speech, and too backward to my duty; and she was still endeavouring to bring me to a greater wariness and strictness in both. If I spoke rashly or sharply it offended her.*[5]

Also in the Puritan tradition, Jonathan's description of his future wife at age thirteen showed that she was, even then, striving to live a perfectly obedient life:

> *She has a strange sweetness in her mind, and a singular purity in her affections, is most just and conscientious in her conduct, and you could not persuade her to do anything wrong or sinful if you would give her half the world, lest she should offend this Great Being.*[6]

Writing to her niece, Anne Steele used her New Year's greeting to urge young Polly to obedience:

O that your mind may be early improved by divine Grace with a sense of your need of this almighty Saviour and that you may be enabled to believe in him and obey him ... don't go to bed one night or come down one morning without praying to God for his Grace.[7]

And writing to a young friend, Frances Ridley Havergal gently rebuked her for repeating someone else's fault:

I write to you as one who is really wanting to follow Jesus altogether, really wanting to live and speak EXACTLY according to His commands and His beautiful example; and when this is the standard, what seems a little thing, or nothing at all, to others, is seen to be sin, because it is disobeying His dear word and not 'following fully.' 'Whatsoever ye would that men should do unto you, do ye even so to them.' Everything which we say of another which we would not like them to say of us (unless said with some right and pure object which Jesus Himself would approve), is transgression of this distinct command of our dear Lord's, and therefore sin, — sin which needs nothing less than His blood to cleanse, sin in which we indulge at our peril and to the certain detriment of our spiritual life. And Jesus hears every word, and sees, to the depth, the want of real conformity to His own loving spirit, from which they spring.[8]

Enjoyment of the love of God

Paradoxically, this stress on submission and obedience led to the deepest joy. Richard Baxter noted of his wife Margaret that despite the hardships of their fugitive lifestyle, she was always singing. We have seen that Anne Steele's life was marked by cheerfulness. Frances Ridley Havergal found that the last years of her life were marked by more or less unbroken enjoyment of the love of God. But in all of church history the description of Sarah Edwards' experience of the love of Christ stands out as one of the most beautiful:

> *...all night I continued in a constant, clear, and lively sense of the heavenly sweetness of Christ's excellent and transcendent love, of his nearness to me, and of my dearness to him... I seemed to myself to perceive a glow of divine love come down from the heart of Christ in heaven, into my heart, in a constant stream, like a stream or pencil of sweet light. At the same time my heart and soul all flowed out in love to Christ, so that there seemed to be a constant flowing and reflowing of heavenly and divine love, from Christ's heart to mine ... I think that what I felt each minute, during the continuance of the whole time, was worth more than all the outward comfort and pleasure which I had enjoyed in my whole life put together ... the glory of God seemed to be all, and in all, and to swallow up every wish and desire of my heart...*[9]

Total consecration

Finally, each of these four women expressed in different ways her desire to consecrate her whole life to God. Margaret Baxter was about twenty years old when she wrote:

> *[God] hath made me desirous this day to give up myself, and all that I have, to him; taking him only for my God and chief felicity.*[10]

She had signed this 'covenant' at much the same time: it was to express the theme of her life.

> *My whole, though broken heart, O Lord!*
> *From henceforth shall be thine:*
> *And here I do my Vow record:*
> *This hand these words are mine.*
> *All that I have, without reserve,*
> *I offer here to Thee.*[11]

Frances Ridley Havergal described her motivation for complete consecration as being a response to the love of Christ:

> *His unchangeableness is the seal upon every attribute; He will be this same Jesus forever. How can mortal mind estimate this enormous promise? How can mortal heart conceive what is enfolded in these words, 'I also for thee'? One glimpse of its fullness and glory, and we feel that henceforth it must be, shall be, and by this grace will be our true-hearted, whole-hearted cry —*

Take myself, and I will be
Ever, only, all for thee![12]

Some may find this devotion too extreme, even fanatical. But these women believed that if God had given his own Son for them, it was not an option to offer praise only during the good times — God was equally worthy of praise when they were going through the most agonizing difficulties. They show that it is possible to live out these words:

Through all the changing scenes of life,
in trouble and in joy,
the praises of my God shall still
my heart and tongue employ.

Notes

Margaret Baxter

Richard Baxter wrote the *Breviate* (a short account) of Margaret's life in 1681. Page references unless otherwise indicated are from the edition of the *Breviate* reprinted in the last century by the Religious Tract Society. Thanks are expressed to the Evangelical Library of London for the use of their copy.

1 J. I. Packer gives her birth date as 1636. But her husband gives her age at death as forty-two (p.65); that would give a birth date of 1639.

2 David L. Edwards, *Christian England*, vol. 2, Eerdmans, 1983, p.314.

3 N. H Keeble, *Richard Baxter: Puritan Man of Letters*, Clarendon Press, Oxford, 1982, p.95.

4 p.5.

5 p.8.

6 p.34.

7 p.33.

8 p.64.

9 James Anderson, *Honourable Women of the Puritan Times*, vol. 2, London, 1862. Reprinted by Soli Deo Gloria Publications, 2001, pp.158–159.

10 p.1.

11 p.36.

12 p.36

13 p.37.

[14] Quoted in J. I. Packer, *A Grief Sanctified: Passing Through Grief to Peace and Joy*, Servant Publications, Ann Arbor, MI, USA, 1997, p.27.

[15] pp.37–38.

[16] p.38.

[17] p.36.

[18] F. J. Powicke, *Richard Baxter under the Cross (1662–1699)*, Jonathan Cape, London, 1927, p.71.

[19] p.40.

[20] N. H. Keeble, *Richard Baxter, Puritan Man of Letters*, p.36.

[21] Full account of this incident provided in Anderson, *Honourable Women*, pp.183–184.

[22] p.43.

[23] p.47.

[24] p.59.

[25] This is omitted from the Religious Tract Society version. Quoted in Packer, *A Grief Sanctified*, p.135.

[26] Packer, *A Grief Sanctified*, p.136.

[27] Packer, *A Grief Sanctified*, p.136.

[28] Baxter's own account of her death, quoted in Powicke, *Richard Baxter under the Cross*, p.275.

[29] p.49.

[30] p.50.

[31] p.57.

[32] p.55.

[33] pp.51–52.

[34] p.52.

[35] p.55.

[36] p.61.

[37] p.47.

[38] p.48.

[39] p.53.

[40] Final verse of "When I survey the wondrous cross," Isaac Watts.

[41] pp.5–7.

[42] pp.9–10.

[43] pp.10–12.

[44] p.24.

[45] pp.16–17.

[46] pp.24–25.

[47] pp.62–63.

[48] This extract is taken from John T. Wilkinson, *Richard Baxter and Margaret Charlton: A Puritan Love-Story*, George Allan & Unwin, London, 1928, pp.177–178.

Sarah Edwards

1 At the beginning of the twentieth century the psychologist William James set out to analyse religious experience from a purely pragmatic point of view. Using real case studies he asked whether religious experience made these individuals more positive and healthy in their everyday life. In the case of Sarah Edwards (among others) he accepted that their religious experience better equipped them for helping other people, and dealing with the uncertainties of life. See William James, *The Varieties of Religious Experience*, Touchstone, New York, 1997.

2 Iain Murray, *Jonathan Edwards, A New Biography*, The Banner of Truth Trust, Edinburgh, 1987, p.82.

3 Murray, *Edwards*, p.83.

4 Sereno E. Dwight, *Memoirs of Jonathan Edwards*, in vol. 1 of the *Collected Writings of Jonathan Edwards*, The Banner of Truth Trust, p.xxxix.

5 Esther Warham Mather was married to the first minister at Northampton. They had three children. When her husband died the church allowed her and the children to go on living in the parsonage. They then called Solomon Stoddard to the ministry, who promptly married Esther. They had twelve children. Solomon lived and ministered until 1729; Esther lived — actively and usefully — until the age of ninety-two. She was a formidably gifted and dynamic woman, and became a legend in her own lifetime.

6 Elisabeth D. Dodds, *Marriage to a Difficult Man: The 'Uncommon Union' of Jonathan and Sarah Edwards*, Westminster Press, Philadelphia, 1975, pp.28–29.

7 Karlson, Carol F. and Crumpacker, Laurie, *The Journal of Esther Edwards Burr 1754–1757*, Yale University Press, New Haven and London, 1984. Letter 21, 13 April 1756, p.192.

8 Dwight, *Memoirs*, p.xlvi.

9 Jonathan Edwards, "Christian Charity, or the Duty of Charity to the Poor Explained and enforced" in Edwards, *Works*, vol. 2, pp.163–173.

10 *Journal of Esther Edwards Burr*, p.54.

11 Edna Gerstner, *Jonathan and Sarah: An Uncommon Union*, Soli Deo Gloria Publications, Morgan, PA, USA, 1995, p.73.

12 Inoculation uses a small dose of smallpox. Lady Mary Wortley Montagu reported its use among Turkish peasant women in the early eighteenth century. Vaccination is the use of cowpox — a more benign form of the disease — and was introduced by Edward Jenner (1749–1823).

13 Murray, *Edwards*, p.441.

14 Dwight, *Edwards*, vol. 1, p.clxxx.

15   *Still the small inward voice I hear,*
That whispers all my sins forgiven,
Still the atoning blood is near
That quenched the flaming wrath of heaven,
I feel the life his wounds impart,
I feel my Saviour in my heart.

16 Wintrop, quoted in Dodds, *Marriage to a Difficult Man*, p.38.

17 Dwight, *Edwards*, vol. 1, pp.xxxix-xl.

18 Dwight, *Edwards*, vol. 1, p. lxii..

19 Dwight, *Edwards*, vol. 1, p.lxiii.

20 Dwight, *Edwards*, vol. 1, p.lxiii.

21 Dwight, *Edwards*, vol. 1, pp.lxiv-lxvi.

22 Dwight, *Edwards*, vol. 1, p.lxvi.

23 Dwight, *Edwards*, vol. 1, p.lxvii.

24 Murray, *Edwards*, pp.485-487.

25 Dwight, *Edwards*, vol. 1, p.clxxix.

Anne Steele

Unless otherwise indicated, references are to documents in the Steele Collection, held in the Angus Library, Regents College, Oxford. Thanks are due to the Principal, Rev. Dr. Paul Fiddes, for permission to quote from these documents, and to the librarian Mrs Sue Mills and also Mrs Jennifer Thorpe for help in locating sources. Thanks are also due to the librarian of the Evangelical Library, London, for allowing me to use the works by Anne Steele held in the library. I am grateful to Dr Karen Smith for allowing me to use her unpublished M.Phil. thesis on the Calvinistic Baptists of Hampshire and Wiltshire.

1 Kenneth Clark, *Civilisation: a Personal View*, BBC, London. 1969, p.269.

2 William Cowper, 'The Task', I, line 749, *Selected Poems*, edited by Nick Rhodes, Carcanet Press, 1988, p.82.

3 STE 3/7 ix. Anne Steele to her parents from Ringwood, 30 December 1745.

4 Baptists in England and Wales were divided from the seventeenth century onwards into two groups — 'Particular' and 'General'. The Particular or 'Calvinistic' Baptists were the larger grouping. They found their origins in the Puritan movement, and believed that God 'elected' believers to salvation. The 'General' Baptists were more

influenced by the Continental 'anabaptists', who believed in universal or 'general' atonement.

5 Edward Compton, *A History of the Baptist Church, Broughton, Hampshire*, Leicester, 1878.

6 The volumes with her entries for the years 1731–1735, 1748–1749 and 1753 to her death in 1760 have survived — the years when her step-daughter Anne was thirteen to eighteen, thirty-one to thirty-two and thirty-six to forty-three. These journals form part of the Steele Collection in the Angus Library.

7 For the information about Broughton Chapel in this section I am indebted to the research done by Dr Karen Smith in "The Community and the Believer: A Study of Calvinistic Baptist Spirituality in some towns and villages of Hampshire and the borders of Wiltshire, c.1730–1830", unpublished M.Phil. thesis for the University of Oxford.

8 The leader or precentor would begin by reading one, two or more lines, then the congregation would sing them; the precentor would read the next line(s), and the congregation would sing them, and so on throughout the hymn. The custom began because many people could not read, and lasted roughly from the seventeenth to the nineteenth centuries. It often meant that singing was monotonous, even dirge-like.

9 Marjorie Reeves, *Pursuing the Muses: Female Education and Nonconformist Culture, 1700–1900*, Leicester University Press, London, 1997. This work includes a discussion of Anne Steele's work and her circle of friends. Marjorie Reeves has done extensive research on the Nonconformists of Hampshire and Wiltshire, much of it based on valuable primary sources from her own family.

10 Michael F. Dixon and Hugh F. Steele-Smith, 'Anne Steele's Health: A Modern Diagnosis', *Baptist Quarterly*, Vol. 32, no. 7, July 1988, pp.351–356.

11 Dixon and Steele-Smith, 'Anne Steele's Health', p.354.

12 Dixon and Steele-Smith, 'Anne Steele's Health', p.354.

13 9th June, 1733. STE. 4/2.

14 Dixon and Steele-Smith, 'Anne Steele's Health', p.351 and notes.

15 STE 1/5.

16 *Christian Hymns*, Evangelical Movement of Wales, 1977, 570.

17 This letter, dated 23 December 1742, from Bourton, is held in the Angus Library. It is addressed on the outside to 'Mrs Steele'. Convention dictated that an unmarried woman of superior social status be addressed as 'Mrs' whether married or single. Anne Steele, though unmarried, was often referred to as 'Mrs Steele'.

266   *In trouble and in joy*

18 STE 3/9 i. Anne Steele to Mary Steele, 7 May 1750.
19 STE 3/9 ii. Anne Steele to Mary Steele from Broughton, 24 October 1751.
20 Reeves, *Pursuing the Muses*, pp.27–28.
21 STE 3/10 ix. Sylviana (AS) to Mary Wakeford, undated.
22 STE 3/9 iii. Anne Steele to Mary Steele, undated.
23 STE 8 i. Anne Steele to William Steele, 27 June 1736
24 STE 3/9 v. Anne Steele to Mary Steele, from Broughton, 4 March 1762.
25 Karen Smith, "The Community and the Believer", pp.241–244.
26 A point cogently argued by her biographer John Shepphard in the Memoir prefixed to the 1863 edition of her *Hymns, Psalms and Poems*.
27 Karen Smith, "The Community and the Believer", p.241f.
28 Theodisia (Anne Steele), *Poems on Subjects chiefly Devotional, in Two Volumes, to which is added a Third Volume consisting of miscellaneous pieces*, Bristol, 1780. Volume 1 included 105 hymns and twenty-eight poems; Volume 2 included fifty-two poems and forty-seven psalms; Volume 3 included seventy-one poems and twenty-one prose pieces.
29 Anne Steele, *Hymns, Psalms and Poems*, ed. John Sheppard, Daniel Sedgwick, London, 1863. This included 144 hymns (some previously appeared as 'poems' in the 1780 collection), thirty-four psalms and forty-eight poems.
30 John Sheppard, in the Memoir of Anne Steele prefixed to the 1863 edition of her *Psalms, Hymns and Poems*, p.v.
31 John Sheppard, Memoir, pp.xiv–xv.
32 Journal of Anne Cater Steele, Angus Library. Whitefield's preaching tours often took him from London to Bristol and Bath, with stops that included Hampshire and Wiltshire. Anne's parents went to hear him on 17 May 1749 at Sarum and 12 June 1752 at Whitchurch.
33 William Steadman was pastor at Broughton from 1791 to 1798. He found the congregation spiritually apathetic, and unsupportive of his efforts to evangelize surrounding villages. Sharon James, 'Perseverance in Evangelism: the example of William Steadman', *Reformation Today*, 161, January/February 1998.
34 This is clearly described in Deryck W. Lovegrove, *Established Church, Sectarian People, Itinerancy and the Transformation of English Dissent, 1780–1830*, Cambridge University Press, 1988. See also extended review article in *Reformation Today*, 119, January/February 1991.
35 STE 3/7 i. Anne Steele to Mrs Steele, 26 September 1729.
36 STE 3/7 ii. Anne Steele to Mrs Steele, 27 September 1734.

37 Quoted in Reeves, *Pursuing the Muses*, p.66.

38 Quoted in Karen Smith, "The Community and the Believer", pp.251-252.

39 Hymn CXXXVIII, *Hymns, Psalms and Poems*, pp.150-151. Originally eight verses. These are the six verses that appear in *Grace Hymns* (no.136).

40 Hymn XC, vv.1,2,4,5, *Hymns, Psalms and Poems*, pp.99-100. (*Christian Hymns*, 476).

41 Hymn XXVI vv.1,5,7,9,11,12, *Hymns, Psalms and Poems*, pp.37-38. (*Christian Hymns*, 323).

42 Reeves, *Pursuing the Muses*, pp.89-90.

43 STE 3/10 iii.

44 STE 3/10 xiii.

45 STE 3/10 ii.

46 Quoted in Reeves, *Pursuing the Muses*, pp.68-69.

47 *Hymns, Psalms and Poems*, p.218.

48 Hymn LXXIV, vv.1,2,8,9, *Hymns, Psalms and Poems*, pp.82-83. (*Christian Hymns*, 758).

49 Hymn LXII, vv.1,3,4,5,6, *Hymns, Psalms and Poems*, pp.70-71. (*Christian Hymns*, 91).

50 STE/8 Anne Steele to William Steele, from Broughton, 5 January 1763. The letter concludes with a note to her brother saying 'I hope you will take care that Polly [his daughter] is as little as possible in the kitchen, I fear the cold will hurt her feet.' Anne then added the postscript (*extract 13*) to Polly.

Frances Ridley Havergal

1 Owen Chadwick, *The Victorian Church*, p.5. See also Donald M. Lewis, *Lighten their Darkness: The Evangelical Mission to Working-Class London, 1828-1860*, Paternoster Press, 2001.

2 Janet Grierson, *Frances Ridley Havergal: Worcestershire Hymnwriter*, Worcestershire, FRH Society, 1979, p.11.

3 Frances Ridley Havergal, *Swiss Letters*, edited by Jane Miriam Crane, James Nisbet, London, 1881, p.47.

4 Frances Ridley Havergal, 'Holiday Work', reproduced in *Swiss Letters*, pp.192-207.

5 Havergal, *Swiss Letters*, p.194.

6 Grierson, *Worcestershire Hymnwriter*, p.2.

7 Maria V. G. Havergal, *Memorials of Frances Ridley Havergal*, London, 1884, p.6.

8 Havergal, *Memorials, 1884*, p.12.

9 Grierson, *Worcestershire Hymnwriter*, p.46.

[10] Havergal, Memorials, 1884, pp.54–55.
[11] Grierson, Worcestershire Hymnwriter, p.87.
[12] Grierson, Worcestershire Hymnwriter, p.190.
[13] Grierson, Worcestershire Hymnwriter, p.102.
[14] Grierson, Worcestershire Hymnwriter, p.103.
[15] Grierson, Worcestershire Hymnwriter, p.79.
[16] Havergal, Memorials, 1884, p.248.
[17] Frances Ridley Havergal, Letters by the Late Frances Ridley Havergal, edited by her sister M.V.G.H., London, James Nisbet, 1885, p.122.
[18] Havergal, Letters, p.121.
[19] Havergal, Swiss Letters, p.198.
[20] Havergal, Swiss Letters, p.163.
[21] Havergal, Swiss Letters, pp.98–99.
[22] Havergal, Swiss Letters, p.282.
[23] Havergal, Swiss Letters, p.74.
[24] Havergal, Swiss Letters, p.296.
[25] Havergal, Swiss Letters, pp.54–55.
[26] Havergal, Swiss Letters, p.70–71.
[27] Havergal, Swiss Letters, pp.246–247.
[28] Havergal, Swiss Letters, p.213.
[29] Havergal, Swiss Letters, p.249.
[30] Havergal, Swiss Letters, p.31.
[31] Havergal, Swiss Letters, pp.335–336.
[32] Havergal, Swiss Letters, p. 340.
[33] Grierson, Worcestershire Hymnwriter, p.169.
[34] Grierson, Worcestershire Hymnwriter, p.169.
[35] T. H. Darlow, Francis Ridley Havergal: a Saint of God, London, 1927, p.37.
[36] Grierson, Worcestershire Hymnwriter, p.139.
[37] Havergal, Memorials, 1884, p.103.
[38] Havergal, Letters, pp.140–141.
[39] Quoted in Darlow, Saint of God, p.39.
[40] Havergal, Letters, p.217.
[41] Grierson, Worcestershire Hymnwriter, p.145.
[42] Havergal, Memorials, 1884, p.106.
[43] Havergal, Memorials, 1884. p.245. The hymn is by Mary Jane Walker (written 1864) for which Frances composed the tune 'Hermas'.
[44] Yet she and her sisters never hesitated to get involved and help individuals when they were in need — there are many people who campaign vigorously for social justice, but who would not think of taking the initiative while on holiday to see if any sick people needed help as they did.

45 Havergal, *Letters*, p.64.
46 Havergal, *Letters*, pp.256–257.
47 Havergal, *Letters*, p.53.
48 Havergal, *Letters*, p.161.
49 Havergal, *Swiss Letters*, pp.17–18.
50 Havergal, *Letters*, p.42.
51 David Bebbington, *Holiness in Nineteenth Century England*, Paternoster Press, 2000, p.19.
52 The doctrine of 'justification by faith alone' can be abused to produce 'easy believism'. And similarly, while there is a sense in which sanctification is 'by faith' this too can be overstated in such a way as to produce passivity. For a Puritan expression of 'sanctification by faith' see the prayer entitled 'Reliance' in *Valley of Vision: A collection of Puritan prayers and meditations*, Banner of Truth Trust, Edinburgh, 2002, p.176.
53 Keswick leaders spoke out against the apathy and half-heartedness of all too many Christians. They stressed the union of the believer with Christ, and the presence of the Holy Spirit. At conversion, the believer is freed from the guilt of sin. They taught that subsequently the believer could be 'consecrated' and freed from the power of sin. In popular thinking, many thought of conversion as recognizing Jesus as Saviour, and sanctification as recognizing Jesus as King or Lord. Christians were sometimes divided into two classes — ordinary ('carnal') Christians, and Spirit-filled Christians, who experienced 'full salvation'. Often it was taught that a one-off 'crisis' experience rather like a second conversion was needed, where the believer would entirely surrender to God, and then find 'rest'. Again, in popular thinking this 'let go and let God' emphasis could mean that sanctification became a passive process of surrendering to God, rather than an active process of fighting against sin. In the week-long Keswick programme, day two was marked out as the day to aim for the delegates to get this blessing. Once this blessing was enjoyed, certainly a believer could lose it through wilful disobedience, but if retained it would result in peace, joy and 'rest'. So the surrendered Christian was lifted up onto a higher level of Christian living, a level of virtually unbroken tranquillity. Consecration led to peace and joy.

The dangers of this view were that sometimes an unbiblical division between first- and second-class Christians became commonplace, an unhealthy passivity replaced a biblical notion of the need to fight sin, and believers were sidetracked into seeking a crisis experience rather than working at the day-to-day reality of Christian obedience. (Although, to be fair, many of those influenced by the Keswick message became extremely active both in home and foreign mission.)

Moreover, the vision of a life of unclouded peace, rest and joy brings the promises of heaven prematurely into life in a fallen world, which will always be a battle. Keswick leaders stopped short of advocating 'sinless perfection' in this life — but the 'two-tier' view of Christianity became standard teaching in some sections of evangelicalism. Moreover, critics pointed out that the tone at Keswick was pietistic, non-controversial, individualistic, and that issues of social justice were ignored. David Smith, for example, sees this emphasis as part 'of a 'general retreat from involvement in social and cultural concerns and the acceptance of a split between the private world, where faith operates, and the public realm, controlled by ideas hostile to religion'. (David W. Smith, *Transforming the World: The Social Impact of British Evangelicalism*, Paternoster Press, 1998, p. 80).

I am indebted here to a paper entitled 'The Keswick Sanctification Theory' given by Geoff Thomas at the 1990 International Baptist Conference in Toronto.

54 Havergal, *Letters*, pp.324–325.

55 This was originally the penultimate verse of a twenty-verse poem entitled 'For New Year's Day, 1874', written at Winterdyne on 23 December 1873. The poem was based on 2 Corinthians 3:18, 'from glory to glory', and the tone was corporate and triumphant. In modern hymnals, a small section has been extracted; the first person plural changed to the first person singular, and the resulting hymn is very individualistic. e.g. 'In full and glad surrender', *Christian Hymns*, 543.

56 *Christian Hymns*, Evangelical Movement of Wales, 1977, 784.

57 Havergal, *Memorials, 1884*, p.53, note. For the tune 'Baca', see *Christian Hymns*, 788.

58 Havergal, *Life Mosaic*, London, 1881, pp.76–77.

59 *Christian Hymns*, 779.

60 *Christian Hymns*, 720.

61 Havergal, *Life Mosaic*, pp.93–94.

62 Frances Ridley Havergal, *Poetical Works*, London, Nisbit & Co., undated, pp.526–527.

63 Havergal, *Poetical Works*, pp.585–586.

64 *Christian Hymns*, 541.

65 Havergal, *Poetical Works*, pp.497–499. *Praise!* includes the second stanza, often omitted from hymnals, and slightly modernizes the words to make it more usable today (*Praise!*, 515).

66 Havergal, *Poetical Works*, pp.28–30.

67 Havergal, *Poetical Works*, pp.487–489.

68 Havergal, *Poetical Works*, pp.716–717.

69 Havergal, *Poetical Works*, pp.714–716.

70 Frances Ridley Havergal, *Life Chords*, 13th edition, London, undated, pp.23,35–36.

71 Frances Ridley Havergal, *Kept for the Master's Use*, reprinted by Baker Book House, USA, 1977, pp.120–128.

72 Frances Ridley Havergal, *Royal Bounty*, reprinted by Baker Book House, USA, 1977, pp.88–89.

73 When I read *Little Pillows* to my own children, I substituted 'Amy' for 'Ethel', 'Ethel' being somewhat dated. They really appreciated the spiritual directness and freshness of each of the children's books written by Havergal which I have read to them.

74 Frances Ridley Havergal, *Little Pillows*, London, Nisbet & Co.

75 Havergal, *Memorials, 1884*, pp.161–162.

76 Havergal, *Letters*, pp.28–29.

77 Havergal, *Letters*, pp.144–146.

78 Havergal, *Swiss Letters*, pp.34–37.

79 Havergal, *Swiss Letters*, pp.286–289.

Conclusion

1 Baxter, *Breviate*, Religious Tract Society, pp.16–17

2 Dwight, *Edwards*, vol. 1, p.clxxix.

3 Hymn LXII, v.3, *Hymns, Psalms and Poems*, pp.70–71. (*Christian Hymns*, 91).

4 Grierson, *Worcestershire Hymnwriter*, p.169.

5 Baxter, *Breviate*, pp.51–52.

6 Dwight, *Edwards*, vol. 1, pp.xxxix-xl

7 STE/8 Anne Steele to William Steele, from Broughton, 5 January 1763. Postscript addressed to Polly.

8 Havergal, *Memorials, 1884*, pp.161–162.

9 Dwight, *Edwards*, vol. 1, p.lxiii.

10 Baxter, *Breviate*, pp.9–10.

11 Wilkinson, *Richard Baxter and Margaret Charlton*, pp.177–178.

12 Havergal, *Kept for the Master's Use*, pp.120–128.

For further reading

Margaret Baxter

J. I. Packer has edited the *Breviate* and included it in his book *A Grief Sanctified: Passing through Grief to Peace and Joy*, Servant Publications, Ann Arbor, MI, USA, 1997.

The *Breviate* was included in John T. Wilkinson, *Richard Baxter and Margaret Charlton: A Puritan Love-Story*, George Adam and Unwin, London, 1928.

On the Puritans:

Erroll Hulse, *Who are the Puritans and what do they teach?* Evangelical Press, 2000.

J. I. Packer, *Among God's Giants*, Crossway, 1990.

Leland Rykin, *Worldly Saints: The Puritans as they really were*, Zondervan, Grand Rapids, USA, 1986.

On Richard Baxter:

N. H. Keeble, *Richard Baxter: Puritan Man of Letters*, Clarendon Press, Oxford, 1982.

Geoffrey F. Nuttall, *Richard Baxter*, Nelson, London, 1965.

F. J. Powicke, *The Reverend Richard Baxter, under the Cross (1662–1691)*, Jonathan Cape, London, 1927.

Soli Deo Gloria Publications (USA) have reprinted a massive four-volume collection of the works of Richard Baxter (reprint 1990) including *The Reformed Pastor, The Saint's Everlasting Rest, Alarm to the Unconverted* and *A Christian Directory*. The Banner of Truth Trust have also reprinted a number of Baxter's works.

Sarah Edwards

Iain Murray, *Jonathan Edwards, A New Biography*, The Banner of Truth Trust, Edinburgh, 1987.

Other works:

Elisabeth D. Dodds, *Marriage to a Difficult Man: The 'Uncommon Union' of Jonathan and Sarah Edwards*, Westminster Press, Philadelphia, 1971.

Jonathan Edwards, *Collected Writings*. Reprinted in two volumes. The Banner of Truth Trust, Edinburgh, 1986. Volume 1 includes the memoir by Sereno E. Dwight, with the full account of Sarah Edwards' religious experience.

Edna Gerstner, *Jonathan and Sarah: An Uncommon Union*, Soli Deo Gloria, Morgan, PA, USA, 1995.

Carol F. Karlsen and Laurie Crumpacker, eds. *The Journal of Esther Edwards Burr, 1754–1757*, Yale University Press, New Haven and London, 1984. (Note that Bentson Press, USA have reprinted a Journal of Esther Burr, but they give no note of its source, and there is a strong question mark as to its authenticity, see Karlsen, p.ix).

Ola Elizabeth Winslow, *Jonathan Edwards 1703–1758, A Biography*. Octagon Books, New York, 1973.

Anne Steele

Marjorie Reeves, *Pursuing the Muses: Female Education and Nonconformist Culture, 1700–1900*, Leicester University Press, London, 1997. This work includes a discussion of Anne Steele's work and her circle of friends. Marjorie Reeves has done extensive research on the Nonconformists of Hampshire and Wiltshire, much of it based on valuable primary sources from her own family.

Anne Steele, *Hymns, Psalms and Poems*, ed. John Sheppard, Daniel Sedgwick, London, 1863. This includes 144 hymns (some previously appeared as 'poems' in the 1780 collection), thirty-four Psalms, and forty-eight poems. This is obviously only available second-hand or through a library.

Frances Ridley Havergal

Several of Frances Ridley Havergal's hymns are in modern hymnals. Some of her books are still available in print or can be found in many church libraries:

Frances Ridley Havergal, *Kept for the Master's Use*, Baker Book House, 1977.

Frances Ridley Havergal, *Royal Bounty*, Baker Book House, 1977.

Other works:

Janet Grierson, *Frances Ridley Havergal: Worcestershire Hymnwriter*, Worcestershire, FRH Society, 1979 (out of print).

Gaius Davies, *Genius, Grief and Grace: A doctor looks at suffering and success*, Christian Focus, Tain, Ross-shire, 2001. This book includes an essay on Frances Ridley Havergal.

Index

Other titles by Sharon James

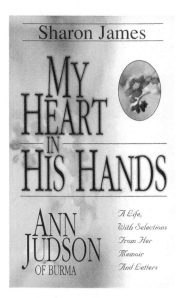

Sharon James

MY HEART IN HIS HANDS

ANN JUDSON OF BURMA

A Life, With Selections From Her Memoir And Letters

'With an abundant use of Ann Judson's journals and letters, Sharon James has given us a beautifully written and moving account of the life of the young nineteenth-century missionary. It is a life which challenges us to renew our own dedication to the spread of the gospel in our day.'
— Elizabeth Catherwood

'This book stands out amongst other biographies of Christian women because Ann Judson makes godliness so attractive and not an unrealizable ideal.'
— Banner of Truth magazine

'An extremely important book in highlighting the pioneering role of women in mission and in revealing the dynamics of a spiritual life founded on God's Word.'
— Evangelicals Now

My Heart in His Hands

Ann Judson of Burma

In October 1810 a twenty-year-old girl in the quiet New England town of Bradford wrote the following words in her journal: 'If nothing in providence appears to prevent, I must spend my days in a heathen land. I am a creature of God, and he has an undoubted right to do with me, as seems good in his sight... He has my heart in his hands, and when I am called to face danger, to pass through scenes of terror and distress, he can inspire me with fortitude, and enable me to trust in him. Jesus is faithful; his promises are precious. Were it not for these considerations, I should sink down with despair...'

Ann Hasseltine had received a proposal of marriage from Adoniram Judson, who was shortly to leave for Asia as one of America's first overseas missionaries. And thus commenced one of the great dramas of church history — a saga of love, courage, suffering and perseverance.

ISBN 0-85234-421-X

God's Design for Women

Biblical Womanhood for Today

Women today are encouraged to think they can 'have it all': career success and family fulfilment at the same time. But these external measures of 'success' leave many feeling inadequate. Sharon James shows that every woman has dignity as she has been made in the image of God, and that every woman can find true fulfilment when she understands, enjoys and fulfils her creation design.

Questions for group discussion are provided.

ISBN 0-85234-503-8

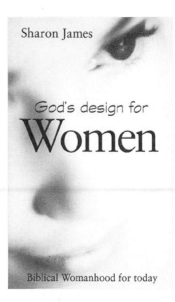

Sharon James

God's design for
Women

Biblical Womanhood for today

'written in a compelling, compassionate, down-to-earth style that is immensely readable'
— Grace Magazine

'If you are going to read one book on biblical womanhood this should be it. Sharon James' book is clearly born out of years of study as well as years of experience in a pastoral context.'
— Themelios (International Journal for Theological and Religious Studies Students)

'essential reading for both women and men in our churches'
— Evangelical Times

'Sharon James is a stimulating thinker. We need more of this calibre of Christian writing at a popular level.'
— Julia Cameron, Head of Communications, IFES (International Fellowship of Evangelical Students)

www.evangelicalpress.org